CW00434091

FLAGS

&

BONES

Ben Wildsmith

Foreword by Jon Gower

Copyright © Ben Wildsmith 2023

All rights reserved.

Print ISBN 978-1-7384231-0-1

The right of Ben Wildsmith to be identified as the author of this work has been asserted by him in accordance with the Copyright Designs and Patents Act 1988

This is a work of satirical and humorous content and commentary written for and published in the public domain by *Nation.Cymru* a news website.

No part of this publication may be reproduced, stored in a retrieval system, or transmitted in any form or by any means without the prior permission in writing of the publisher. Nor be otherwise circulated in any form or binding or cover other than that in which it is published and without a similar condition being imposed on the subsequent purchaser.

Published by

Llyfrau Cambria Books, Wales, United Kingdom.

Cambria Books is an imprint of

Cambria Publishing Ltd.

Discover our other books at: www.cambriabooks.co.uk

Ben Wildsmith was born in Birmingham. A weekly columnist for *Nation.Cymru*, he has been an aspiring musician since he was 15, and also works with homeless people in Cardiff. He's a Hay Festival Writer at Work. Ben's enthusiasms include procrastination and footnotes. He lives in Rhondda Fach with his wife, Susie, and a gnawing sense of dread.[1]

---

[1] Not caused by Susie.

CONTENTS

Foreword

Ben Wildsmith's writing is some of the sharpest around. He wields sentences as if they are bright scalpels, cutting deep into the flesh of his subjects, without any recourse to anaesthetic.

It's often sharp enough to work like a microtome, that scientific tool that shaves specimens thin enough to set beneath a microscope slide. Because Wildsmith *examines*, scrutinises, holds people to account even as he holds up any tissue of lies to the glare of the light, to the arc lamp of examination.

It can be angry writing too, fuelled by a grave sense of injustice at a world which doesn't seem to care, or at least not care half enough about people who need more support from society not less. Much as do writers such as the *Guardian*'s Marina Hyde, Wildsmith can turn a politician into a deserving target, then take aim with a steady hand and a gimlet eye, puncturing their arguments like peppershot.

I'm hugely glad to have played a very small part in the story of *Flags & Bones*. Ben and I were once sitting in a Cardiff pub discussing life, writing and rugby when I suggested he might like to write about a sport that's clearly so near to his heart. It's also a subject about which he is both deeply knowledgeable and white-heat passionate.

He duly delivered, the first of many vivid accounts that have graced the online pages of *Nation.Cymru*. They tell of visits to rugby clubs full of sterling characters and insufficent fibrillators for those heart attack moments watching a game. He documents old, old allegiances to both club and country and details scores settled in mud or on the modern acres of Astroturf.

He then broadened the field of his weekly column's enquiry, taking in the ills and injustices of modern life and taking on those who are meant to guard against them, in a sense to level the playing fields.

As a fellow writer I'd have to say that Ben is enviably good, forever upping his game and delivering high-octane opinion set within coruscating prose. Sharp, yes, but compassionate too, caring about unfairness much as he does about the words that shine brilliantly through.

Jon Gower

Introduction

When I first started writing these columns for *Nation.Cymru*, I had the feeling of being a newly qualified driver. I had wanted to do this so badly, and for so long, but each keystroke was an oncoming lorry that could wipe me out if I was careless for a second. The temptation is to drive slowly and keep well away from the centre line.

For a start, I was writing about international rugby – the M4 at rush-hour of topics here in Wales. It doesn't matter how much you think you know about this glorious, infuriating game, someone in the Post Office queue knows more. If this were Germany, we would have a compound word for the dawning realisation that you have just offered your opinion on Saturday's game to a man who played for Wales A in 1982.

Not that lived experience is a passport to respect, either. I was on Twitter the other week and saw a row erupt between a legendary, two-code international and an opinionated nobody over league structures. By the end of it, the international had been blocked by the keyboard warrior who was 'tired of his childish grasp of the issue.'

Fortunately, there's a route out of all this, which is to accept you know nothing and try to convey how the game *felt* for everyone watching. The emotional sway that rugby still holds over a big chunk of the population is etched on to the faces of people in pubs and clubs with every final whistle. How this manifests is a reliable indicator as to how a person deals with life in general. There are, I reckon, two archetypes and I grew up with one of each.

My mum would lose it altogether in the final quarter of a tight game. She'd be screaming xenophobic abuse at the telly, running out of the room because she couldn't face watching crucial kicks at goal, and banging pots and pans around in the kitchen if Wales lost.

My grandad, on the other hand, would quietly darken as matches slipped away from us. Insisting that it was 'only a game', his educated commentary would slow to a trickle, finally atrophying into occasional muttering.

'*Blydi* clowns.'

I see this in clubs I visit across the nation as we offer up our personalities in service of the impossible dream. After two consecutive defeats, none of us are ever going through this again. The game is over in Wales, and we are fools for clinging on to past glory when the future is zip wires and bucket hats. That's it, we're out. Then the team pulls off an unlikely victory and the clubs are bouncing again. The only thing I'm certain of in life is that when I die, I'll know the result of the last international and hold an opinion about who should be in the back row for the next one. It'll be wrong, of course.

According to lore, when Nye Bevan was asked about his brother running for election to the Welsh Rugby Union's committee, he shook his head.

'It's not something I'd do.'

'Why?'

'I'm not that interested in politics.'

When, after some pleading on my part, I was permitted to write a weekly political column, it carried none of the anxiety inherent to my rugby pieces. If you find yourself in disagreement with a well-known political figure nowadays, there is a better than evens chance that you're in the right.

Whatever your political persuasion, we can all agree that the current line-up of *I'm an Otherwise Unemployable, Incompetent Narcissist... Get Me Out of Here and on to a GB News Sofa* is the most dispiriting gang of social inadequates we've seen in our lifetimes.

The behaviour on display at PMQs would result in a clip round the ear were it to be tried anywhere that decent people gather. Skirting ever closer and into criminality, our politicians conspire with the client media to act out a pantomime in which actual governance is barely attended to in favour of naked careerism and, not infrequently, personal enrichment.

The truth is fatal in this world. If a politician hits social media after a few too many we sometimes have a glimpse of what they actually think. To watch our leaders recoiling in horror at notions they privately agree with, whether from Lee Anderson or Diane Abbott, is to experience dishonesty not as a failing but an assumed virtue.

So, to hell with them. In my day job, I work alongside people trying honestly to protect the vulnerable from awful decisions made by those in power. We see the hopelessness and pain that rains down from Westminster, occasionally sheltered by the flimsy umbrella of Cardiff Bay. We try to mop up the flood when it isn't.

So, facing a blank page every Saturday and looking for a politician who deserves a booting is a pleasure, a privilege, and far easier than it should be.

You can't be angry all the time, though, not if you want to stay married. There's 'what I did on my holidays' pieces here, some bits of whimsy, and the odd venture into the philosophical wilderness, from which I'm frequently rescued by readers arriving in the comments section like St Bernard dogs on the Matterhorn.

Nation.Cymru has published them all, often to my astonishment, and with only the gentlest of editorial raised eyebrows. That readers have given me their time is thrilling beyond my imagination.

Diolch yn fawr.

Ben Wildsmith, August 2023

Flags, Bones and Old Smokey

7 May 2023

Driving up the valley to Lidl in Tylorstown on the night before the Coronation, the rain intensifies, drumming on the windscreen like a warning. It's further to go than the one in Porth but my family lived up there once and supermarket shopping is less tedious if you're being haunted.

Nobody's on the streets. Bank holiday weekend you'd expect a few out on Friday night, even in this weather. Everyone's indoors, making their own worlds.

A group of kids is sat on top of the trolleys, not causing any trouble nor serving any purpose. Lidl is somewhere to go, I suppose. Underneath them, in 1896, 57 miners died along with 80 horses. Empires are built on bones that outlast them.

When I was little, my grandfather, who grew up here, would speak of royalty with a searing contempt that made it memorable. It wasn't the affectionate pisstaking of my Brummie relatives, but serious, controlled rage that such a thing could exist. Carrying shrapnel from El Alamein, and chalk dust from 50 years in a Birmingham classroom, he wasn't having any of it.

'Useless parasites.'

A man comes out cradling 12 tins of Lidl's own lager in his arms. Another week over.

It's becoming harder to be a ray of light these days, don't you think? Emerging from the collective trauma of the Pandemic, there were some who spoke of 'building back better' as if it had been a salutary curse from above, sent to bring us to our senses. Instead, we've rolled and tumbled down a scree slope of boarded-up pubs and nuclear threats with bent politicians and global tyrants at our backs. A few extra tins seems more sensible than it used to.

I shouldn't drink nowadays, but I want a bit of something nice this evening. I've spent all week searching round Cardiff for one of the homeless people we support at work. He walked out of a secure ward without his medication and the police were very busy this week. We found him in the end; it was a worry, though.

The king prawns are marked down by 30% and I love prawns, but discounted seafood never seems like a good idea. There are only three of us in here shopping under the painfully bright lights. The checkout staff are unpacking stock in the aisles, waiting to go home.

Driving back, the light's dimming further and the rain is just spitting, more of a complaint now. A solitary house displays Union flag bunting across its railings. Dwarfing its neighbours, the house stares over the valley to Old Smokey – the coal tip. Last week there were engineers up there prodding at it to see if there was any danger of another slippage. The last one careened harmlessly down the mountain into the river, leaving a black tongue draped behind it on the slope. If Old Smokey itself came down though, well, that would be different. It sits up there like it owns the place, covered in greenery. It's not real though, just playing at being a natural feature. It has no foundations. It's a lie.

Princess Mick

11 December 2022

When Prince Harry married RMT leader Mick Lynch back in 2016, there had been some concern that the union would meet resistance from less progressive members of the public and, indeed from older members of the royal household. Those fears turned out to be unfounded as the nation took Princess Mick to its hearts in a display of civic unity unrivalled since Kylie Minogue arrived on a giant flip-flop at Arthur Scargill's state funeral.

Many people hoped that the nation's unbounded admiration for the royal couple heralded a new era of openness for a country that had struggled to come to terms with its legacy of suboptimal industrial relations. The late Duke of Edinburgh reportedly adored Princess Mick, writing encouraging personal notes to the newcomer, and affectionately reminding him of what happened to Wat Tyler.

The Great British Public, meanwhile, took to social media to express their unanimous love for Harry and Mick. Many, to this day, are unaware of Mick's socialism. And those who noticed it felt that his Marxist proclivities enriched the nation.

'Edward VIII was a Nazi and Diana liked Duran Duran. Live and let live, I say,' Royalist Ron Staunch told the *Daily Mail* from his mock Tudor hovel in Essex.

'Just because he's a left footer, it doesn't mean he can't embody a hierarchical structure of power and privilege in such a way that the oppressed remain so dazzled by displays of opulence that they forget their own poverty. Some of my best friends are anarcho-syndicalists.'

So, imagine the sense of betrayal when it was revealed this

week that Princess Mick was hell-bent on ruining Christmas. At a time when the nation was shivering under the thin blanket of a £66-per-month cost-of-living payment, the former national treasure was observed setting light to a manger at his $450 million Montecito ranch.

Christmas has endured several *anni horribili* of late. Ever since Sadiq Khan persuaded the United Nations to classify the winter festival as a war crime, it has become routine for families to be herded into re-education camps for the festive season. Here, under the guidance of Gary Lineker and Just Stop Oil, they are encouraged to celebrate a non-gendered, vegan Ecomas. *Morecambe and Wise* is forbidden viewing.

Old traditions are hard dying, though, and if you know where to look you can still see underground expressions of the old Christmas. In Cardiff's St David's Centre, for instance, they have managed to evade the authorities and play Mariah Carey's 'All I Want For Christmas Is You' 500 times a day since late September, in a powerful statement of spiritual opposition to Khan and Lineker's New Order.

That Christmas still exists at all is, of course, thanks to the bravery of our fallen leader, Boris Johnson. Boris, as everybody acknowledges, got the big decisions right and none was more important than his valiant sacrifice of a few hundred thousand grannies to save Christmas. Princess Mick would do well to study Boris' example if he is ever to recover the affection of the nation.

These are uncertain times and leadership is thin on the ground. Only this week we have lost the wise guidance of the statesman Matt Hancock, who has chosen to lend his wisdom and expertise to media interests in the private sector. As patriots, we are tested as never before, and I am confident that I speak for all of you in expressing the devastation we felt when the Duchess of Cambridge put that penalty over the bar against France last night. For the epitome of elegance and grace to be mocked by fate in such a stark manner caused me to question the existence of a benign deity.

But never mind, we have our faith to rely upon: Kate good/Meghan bad, Business good/unions bad – and anyone who says different is insulting our late Queen.[1]

---

[1] Writing this left me wondering how *Daily Mail* columnists manage to assemble similar stuff so frequently. Forcing information into this strange shape is exhausting.

Let Them Eat Turnips

26 February 2023

When you hurl yourself from an airplane and find that your parachute has been packed by a Year Nine student on work experience who only got the placement because his dad financed the company, there must, presumably, be some time to reflect. Before landing on the airfield with a desultory thud, you are granted a while to take in the scenery. You might notice a sympathetic glance from a passing seagull; or discern the changing air pressure as blood trickles from your ears. If it's a local adventure, you might even be able to pick out the rooftop of your own home, imagining the devastation that is about to be overwhelm your loved ones on account of this folly.

Or… you might look up at the plane, descending calmly towards the runway and shout,

'See! They're affected by gravity too. It's nothing to do with jumping out of the plane!'

I have a peculiar knack of being out of the country for signal moments of national turmoil. In 1997, I was in an Egyptian restaurant in Arizona when the owner came over and, standing to attention, sombrely announced that Princess Diana had been killed in Paris. Watching through a media-lens as Britain seemed to descend into a pantomime of performative grief was a strange and disconcerting experience. The media, though, focuses on what suits its narrative, and nothing remotely sensible made its way on to American TV screens.

I'm writing this from Morocco and find myself with the irresistible opportunity to mimic the asinine trolling of Brexiteers right back at them. During the last produce shortage, my Facebook feed filled up with photos of groaning supermarket shelves as gleeful Farageists employed their own brand of rapier wit to dismiss the situation as Remoaner exaggeration.

'Oh no, nothing to be found in the Cowbridge Waitrose!!!!!!!!!!! What will we do?!!!!!!' Followed by a stream of crying emojis and Union flags.

People I somehow know were doing this on a daily basis: taking photos of supermarkets in areas that had food to prove that reports of shortages in other areas were propaganda.

If I'm lucky enough to survive into retirement, I rather hope that life offers me richer diversions than photographing cauliflowers in the service of Jacob Rees-Mogg, but I somehow doubt it. Because here, as the sun streams through on to the terrace of my Essaouira apartment, I have been gripped by a peculiar obsession: tomatoes.

I've never eaten so many! I've been here a week now and at Chez Zak, he knows the routine.

'Ah, Monsieur Tomate!'

'Salaam, Zak!'

'Votre tajine de sardines et tomates avec des tomates supplémentaires, une salade de tomates et du jus de tomates. Bon appétit!'

I'm here to tell you that Thérèse Coffey's cunning plan to persuade you that bad weather in Morocco is to blame for this week's special at Dominos being 'The Baldrick'[1] has been rumbled. There's a handcart piled high with juicy ones within

---

[1] She'd advised us to replace tomatoes with local vegetables…in February.

sight of me right now!²

This week's intervention by the Marie Antoinette of root vegetables is another feature to notice on our descent to the ground. Nobody has suggested any strategies for actually acquiring the produce we want; all that matters is that we take a side on why we don't have it. If the reason becomes glaringly obvious, then we're informed that it was an outrageous indulgence for us to expect such things in the first place. Conveniently, this latter argument can be shackled to environmental concerns, allowing Brexiteers to label anyone upset that they can't have spaghetti for tea a hypocrite in the wider battle between selfishness and reason. This despite their stated aim to shred environmental regulations.

God knows how much further there is to fall. Moments of peril tend to be experienced in slow motion, so the ground might be rising more quickly than we hope. Either way, it's hard to remember a day in our recent history that held more hope than the last. Both major parties promise 'growth' as the nebulous cure for our ills, as if shouting 'weightlessness' will reverse the force of gravity. I'll be back in the Rhondda next week to see what's left in the fridge.

---

[2] No there isn't; I've inserted that line for the book in place of the photo I took of the handcart. I'm in the Rhondda and, whilst the fridge does contain four tomatoes, they are not, as far as I know, Moroccan.

Woke Wales and Government by Conspiracy

30 April 2023

You're woke, I'm woke, avocados are woke, the cat is woke, those mountains are woke. Everything is woke except the person calling them woke.

When the right-wing opinion factories of the US and their subsidiaries in London discovered this African-American term for acquiring political awareness, it offered them a single syllable signifier with which to mislead their audience about seemingly anything.

Once captured as a pejorative term, it has no gradation or nuance. Nothing is 'a bit woke', or 'too woke', things are either condemned as woke or they are not. In recent weeks, the Wokefinders General of British politics have turned their attention to Wales and, unsurprisingly, a positive result has been returned.

The choice to use the Welsh name for a national park is the perfect playing field for the game these people play, and the seemingly innocuous nature of the issue is key to their success. Nobody went on hunger strike or set anything on fire to demand the removal of the English name for Bannau Brycheiniog; it was a marketing decision. In two weeks, however, it has been inflated into an international story upon which everybody is supposed to have an opinion. The mechanics of this are familiar. An obscure issue is identified – often the utterance of a minor celebrity or unknown American academic – then presenters from outlets like GB News, Talk TV and the *Daily Mail* focus on it relentlessly, ensuring that it appears widely in social media feeds. Once this cut-through is achieved, the issue then qualifies as a topic about which public figures can be questioned. The obscurity of the topic allows those shaping a confected debate to play fast and loose with the facts, confident that so few people will know them that they won't be called on it.

This is the point we reached this week when Rishi Sunak told BBC Wales that he will be continuing to say 'Brecon Beacons' when he's on the drive to his static caravan in Borth.[1] Professing to be a 'big supporter of the Welsh language and culture', the PM noted that despite this, 'most people' would continue to use the English term for the park. And here is the rub. 'Most people' didn't know they had any opinion at all about this until it became the seasonal replacement for 'Lefties are cancelling Christmas'. The 'most people' that Sunak is talking to are a small number of swing voters in English constituencies whom he hopes can be distracted from the state of the UK's governance with the threat of a generalised external threat. See also, Sir Keir Starmer's 'deeply patriotic' Labour Party.

The Daily Mail et al. are fond of commencing headlines about the latest example of wokery with the word 'now'. Here's the Brownies on the receiving end of this tactic in March:

> **Now the Brownies are dragged into a woke row as 'God' is removed from the lyrics of a camp song to ensure Girlguiding movement is 'inclusive of all religions'.**

The effect of this is to suggest that something is retreating in the face of a concerted threat. In the same way that 'hordes' of migrants are 'invading' Kent, a 'woke mob' is besieging everything from traditional children's pastimes to beloved beauty spots. Repeated on a daily basis, with a rotating roster of targets, the headlines announce new encroachments into areas of life to which 'most people' hold some kind of emotional attachment.

---

[1] Since burned down by Carol Vorderman.

Each day, according to the *Mail*, new territory is lost. NOW it's the Brownies, NOW it's the Brecon Beacons, NOW it's *Little Britain*, NOW it's hardworking publicans with an innocent penchant for golliwogs.

In the face of such an onslaught, consumers of these stories are ripe for the suggestion that someone must be behind it all. And this is how the payoff works. Once everyone from the PM down has been required to pick a side on an inflated non-issue, the big reveal can be made that 'extremists' who oppose the UK government are behind whatever change is being proposed. Moreover, these infidels have links to people for whom YOU might be considering voting. Here's the *Daily Mail* again explaining how changing the name of a national park should result in the reversal of devolution:

REVEALED: Woke renaming of the Brecon Beacons that has infuriated millions was masterminded by a Corbyn-loving Twitter troll and Welsh separatist whose vile posts tell Margaret Thatcher to 'burn in hell' and call Conservative ministers 'Tory scum'.

The Woke Scare is a creature of the first-past-the-post electoral system. UK governments enjoy virtually no checks and balances on their power whilst in office. This luxury becomes a curse when things go so wrong in the country that failures can no longer be denied. Under these circumstances, the last bullet in the gun is to try to pin general discontent on minor, emotive issues that can be ascribed to public institutions. The Welsh and Scottish governments, the Civil Service, the Judiciary, the BBC, the RNLI, the National Trust etc. have all been lumped in together with the Duchess of Sussex and strikers to create the impression that the catastrophic decline in British living standards is not the fault of those who have been running the country for the last 13 years, but the result of their sterling efforts being undermined by a network

11

of mysteriously powerful dissidents.

Government by conspiracy theory didn't end well for Donald Trump, and polls suggest that that it won't work for Sunak's Conservatives either. The truth remains, however, that the decision will lie not with the general will of the people but with a handful of voters in swing constituencies to whose assumed prejudices the Establishment has relentlessly pandered.

Six Nations Anticipation

4 February 2022

It's bad enough every year, isn't it? You drag yourself through the January gloom, fearing the Christmas credit card statement, with just one glimmer of light on the horizon: the Six Nations. But then it's upon you, and like Dry January, Veganuary and your gym membership, it can all seem a bit much.

So, frankly, you could do without daily reports that 45 squad members are injured, or the entire rugby-playing population of Cardiff has been marooned by pestilence in Africa – it beats high winds on the Severn Bridge as an excuse, I suppose.

I've come to Wattstown RFC to see them play Treherbert in League 3 East B. Walking across the bridge from the clubhouse to the ground, the drizzle intensifies, we must take extra precautions against the 'Rhondda variant'[1], so I put on my hat and press on through the park.

There's a fair few here for the game and before the teams emerge on to the pitch the sun breaks through over the mountain, as if to reward us. Wattstown go top of the table if they win this, and they seem intense. While Treherbert amble on cheerfully, the home side form a huddle and demand the best of each other.

'Standards, boys, standards!'

It's a tense affair, and Treherbert take an early lead against the run of play. Their coach is running the line, terrier-like,

---

[1] The press was still full of warnings about 'variants of concern', and a return to lockdown if one took hold. Writing about sport had to be more nuanced as fortunes on the pitch were shaded by nervous relief that we could enjoy the game at all.

shouting advice to players: 'Cut back in, like I showed you…', whilst keeping up a running commentary for the spectators. The Wattstown captain is unconcerned.

'All we need here is some accuracy boys, don't try to win the game in 10 minutes.'

Right enough, patient play from Wattstown sees them overhaul the lead, prompting the Treherbert supporters to become more vocal.

'Come on Tre, let's get something about us!'

'Throw the ball in straight, that hooker's got eyes like Ben Turpin!'

Half-time arrives with the game in the balance and Jay-Z blaring incongruously from the Tannoy. Once again, he's failed to make it in person, though, having got on the wrong bus at Porth.

The second half brings a pair of yellow cards for Treherbert, and the assembled settle into a familiar routine.

'Referee, you're a disgrace to the green jersey!'

Then, when a player is virtually brained in a ruck,

'He'll be alright, it's only his head!'

As the sun dips and the players tire, controversy warms us: the luxury of caring about something that isn't life or death for a change.

Wattstown 21, Treherbert 17.

In the clubhouse after the game, I ask around for views on next week.[2]

---

[2] One older gentleman demanded proof that I wasn't from the English press before he'd talk to me at all. There's only so much social upheaval that can be effected by a single pandemic.

Dennis says we could do with the tournament being delayed. There's general agreement that the regional scene is a shambles and the national team will suffer for it.

John thinks Ireland will build on their strong showing in the autumn.

'You don't beat New Zealand by accident.'

Neil reckons Wales will be third 'if we're lucky' but fancies France to edge Ireland overall.

Reuben, 13, thinks long and hard about how Wales might prosper against the odds.

'Maybe some magic from the wings, Zammit or Josh,' he offers, echoing generations before him who looked to Shane, Ieuan, Gerald, Dewi or Ken to rescue us from the margins with something otherworldly.

Everyone thinks Dan Biggar is the right choice for skipper.

'I had him down as a Prima donna, but he's improved,' says Ian. 'At least he's sure of his place.'

There's an air of resignation about it all that goes beyond the usual stoicism with which we protect ourselves from painfully misplaced expectations of the team. If they come third, it would be alright, no shame in it.

Anyway, the boys from Treherbert have the Scotland game to look forward to. The club has had an exchange going on with Stobswell RFC in Dundee for 50 years and they'll be down for a game on the Friday night before the international. The beers are flowing now, and two lads, for reasons unknown, have turned up dressed as Pinocchio and Geppetto. We'll worry about Wales next week. Here in Wattstown, rugby is back and humming along like a tune we all know. We've missed it.

Look at Me, Ma, I'm King of the World!

12 June 2022

Confidence is an elusive ally in life, isn't it?[1] I pad downstairs at six each morning accompanied by a gnawing dread that the day's demands will be beyond me. As the kettle boils, a kaleidoscopic whirl of unpaid bills, monthly appraisals and weekly timesheets conspire with inexplicable aches and nausea to suggest that the next few hours will include destitution, hospitalisation and death before lunch. Only after a second cuppa do I risk opening my emails and squinting at them as Radio 4 relates the wider chaos of existence. The relentless ghastliness of the news offers comfort as I close the laptop and select which of my two pairs of Primark loafers look most likely to survive the day. After all, I may have 'once again failed to input client outcomes on the master system', but I haven't, for instance, ordered £4bn of useless PPE that I now have to burn, nor failed to notice that I was at my own birthday party.[2] My life may be a bin fire but it's more manageable viewed alongside the inferno of current affairs.

Once I'm in the Honda Jazz and chugging up the hill to Trebanog, things begin to brighten. The swarm of cars converging on Llantrisant underlines our antlike anonymity and I'm soothed by the notion that whatever we all do today when we get to Cardiff, none of the rest of us will know or care about it. On a stretch of dual carriageway, the driver of a gold-wrapped Range Rover becomes frustrated with the Jazz's rate of progress in the outside lane and decides to undertake. Unfortunately, this

---

[1] Particularly when you're writing the first sentence of a political column that you're desperately hoping will be commissioned weekly. Deep breaths, Ben, deep breaths.

[2] Boris, obvs.

coincides with a particularly preachy episode of *Thought for the Day,* and I express my disdain by gradually increasing speed until the Jazz starts shuddering and the Range Rover has to brake lest it ploughs into the back of a number 132 bus. Victory assured, I slip into the inside lane behind the bus and smile in the mirror.

In the office, tea is on the go and we're all cheerfully moaning, as is our birthright. Of *course* there's another bullshit meeting about protocol this afternoon, it's not as if we haven't got enough on our plates, is it? And in companionable discontent, we lend each other the solidarity required to propel us through the day. We'll be alright.

Confidence, for most of us, is hard-won and fleeting. We need it to get things done but are mistrustful of those who seem to possess too much of it. A surfeit of confidence suggests something aberrant in a person's character or upbringing. How, for instance, do you think you'd have fared at home if, as a child, you had expressed the ambition to be 'world king'? I'm guessing my parents would have laughed the first time, told me to shut up the second and, this being the 1970s, employed mild violence had I persisted beyond that. They might well have pointed to the state of my bedroom and asked how it augured for the world's fortunes under my absolute monarchy. If anybody has evidence of Alexander Boris de Pfeffel Johnson keeping an immaculate childhood bedroom, please send it to me, along with a copy of Ozzy Osborne's Duke of Edinburgh Award.

The confidence of others, though, requires more than the blithe assumption that one is fabulous. Rewind to when I arrived at the office. If a sizeable proportion of my moaning colleagues had been so dissatisfied with me that they had demanded a vote on whether I should be summarily dismissed, I reckon it would have given me pause for thought. *How have I gone so wrong*, I'd have fretted, as they excluded me from the tea round.

A confidence trick is a trick in which someone deceives you by telling you something that is not true, often to trick you out of money. – collinsdictionary.com

If, when they had their vote, it turned out that 41% of them wanted me on the first coach out of Dodge, I'd at least have asked if there was anything I could improve. I emphatically would not announce that it was an 'extremely good, positive, conclusive, decisive result and get my creepy mate to call it a 'handsome victory' that proved I was beyond reproach and should carry on smashing it out of the park in perpetuity. That said, I don't drive a gold-wrapped Range Rover, do I?

So, what is it that fuels the limitless self-regard that abounds in Westminster? That 11 out of 12 lavatories in Parliament recently tested positive for cocaine can be attributed to residue from visiting popstars during the Cool Britannia period of the late '90s. Our current politicos are in the grip of a more pernicious addiction: public service. It starts innocently enough. Perhaps you give over a Saturday afternoon to open a local fete. Obviously, the local paper is there to report it and you are congratulated for your selflessness. Feels good, doesn't it? Maybe a constituent has a tax problem. It won't hurt to call the Revenue for him, will it? Word gets around that you're a bloody good bloke and not like the rest at all. How right they are! From childhood you have insisted that you are special, it's this unshakeable belief that has propelled you past all criticism to where you are today. Finally, the people have recognised you as who you are: a vessel for their hopes and dreams. When you prosper, they prosper.

And that's how they are. When Keir Starmer has a shave in the morning, he isn't just having a shave. Oh no, he's shaving for the working man, so that the Tory papers can't undermine the cause by accusing him of scruffiness. You can try this mindset out for yourself. Going down the pub for a skinful? You need to be in touch with the common man. Buying a car you can't afford? People need to know you support aspirational values.

Once you have fused your own fortunes with those of the public, your every action becomes an act of philanthropy and every detractor an enemy of the people. Resign? What have the poor people done to deserve that?

There were points this week when Johnson looked like he might go full-Trump and dismiss representative democracy altogether. He seemed to suggest that the Tory majority was attributable solely to him, with MPs relegated to courtiers who served at his whim and favour. During his 'let's not be hasty, I'll probably go but why don't you take a few months to think it over' non-resignation speech on Thursday, the veil slipped on his conception of British democracy. Contemplating a future without himself at the helm, the PM conceded that 'our brilliant and Darwinian system' will produce another leader. And this, fellow plebs, is at the heart of our woes. Our leaders don't even *imagine* that they are vessels for the values of the poor saps who vote for them. No, they believe that innate strength determines their elevated positions in society, and elections are merely the playing field upon which they demonstrate their prowess.

Johnson's eventual downfall was triggered by the alleged sexual misconduct of the man who coordinated 'Operation Save Big Dog' around the time Rishi began designing his website. As the field assembles to contest the succession, we should be very careful not allow relief at the passing of one large mammal to neuter scrutiny of the next. Integrity is a fine sounding word; so was sovereignty.[2]

---

[2] I'm fond of a portentous final sentence. My imagined reader is a 25-year-old Catherine Deneuve, inexplicably travelling in time to enjoy *Nation.Cymru* and concluding, 'He is deep, this Wildsmith…'

Big in Ukraine

28 August 2022

Dragging yourself back to work after an agreeable holiday is always a pain, isn't it? You need to ease yourself in gently, selecting tasks that don't demand too much of your psyche, half of which remains convinced that you'll be back in your favourite taverna at lunchtime, dipping bits of fried squid in tzatziki and blowing the foam off a pint of Mythos.

It's time to rearrange your desk or offer to fetch the coffee for your colleagues. Anything, in fact, to delay opening your emails, because in there will be all the 'WHERE ARE YOU?' demands from people whose very existence is what ushered you to the airport in the first place.

For Boris Johnson, life is writ large, so while you fear an email from Karen in accounts marked 'urgent' and opt to avoid it by having a vape with the security guy out by the bins, our errant PM is dodging 67.3 million emails titled 'For the Love of God, Save Us!' by addressing the Ukrainian Parliament.

I have a colleague at work who transforms into Roadrunner at 5.15 p.m. each Friday, such is her determination to reach her caravan in Narbeth for the weekend. For some time now Kyiv has been Boris Johnson's happy place. When he signed on for the prime-ministering gig, events in Ukraine were exactly the sort of thing he thought he'd be doing. Bestriding the world stage, old boy! I absolutely guarantee that, as a child, he had a map laid out with battalions and tank formations that he could move around with a stick.

So, it's jolly convenient having Kyiv a short hop away when he's in danger of having to engage with hordes of plebs banging on about their gas bills or excrement on the beach. In Kyiv, hopeful bluster is understandably appreciated at the moment, and they are rather too busy to drill down into the substance of anything Johnson says. All he needs to do is be there and give it Boris for the cause.

The martial rhetoric which was received as grossly offensive during the pandemic is just the ticket for this performance. Remember when we were going to 'take it on the chin' at the outset of Covid? He just needed the right audience.

This week he was presented with the Ukrainian Order of Liberty before having a plaque to him unveiled on the 'alley of bravery' outside the parliament building. In return, he reassured the Ukrainians that while the UK might be facing utter ruin this winter we didn't mind as it was in the service of facing down Putin's evil. Remember that when you're defrosting your granny next month. This is all rather like watching some innocent newcomer start a relationship with your psychopathic ex. There is a compelling case for leaving an anonymous note under Volodymyr Zelensky's windscreen wiper – 'When he says he wants to level you up, don't believe him…'

For all Johnson's reluctance to leave office, this final stretch of his tenure has been very much on his own terms: on holiday for most of it, hosting an extravagant party to wind up the puritans, ignoring anything that looks like hard work while, instead, flying in helicopters and impersonating Churchill. I suppose having 'got the big decisions right' he can afford to take his hand off the tiller and enjoy the trappings of his success as the UK prospers. Thanks Chief!

The difference between you and Johnson is that you will eventually open Karen's email and deal with whatever foul task she has for you. Firstly, you're too decent not to and secondly, you've got a mortgage to pay. In short, you're engaged with reality. Johnson, and by extension the UK, has been running on fantasy for years. From Brexit to our 'world beating' Covid response to decimated public services and rampant tax avoidance, we refuse to open the email. This winter, consequence is coming knocking and no amount of faux patriotism, jubilees, football, *Great British Bake Off*s or Captain Tom is going to dissuade it from breaking down the door and demanding we face it. Here in Wales, we'll look after each other, we always do. Come spring, though, we need to start holding the fantasists to account, because this has gone on long enough.

Gaslit

19 June 2022

If there's one thing that grinds Priti Patel's gears more than the exploitation of innocent refugees by trafficking gangs, it's people who disrespect the vibrant, democratic values of Rwanda. Ms Patel, who holidays in the Golan Heights, simply cannot abide the sort of small-minded bigot who allows the genocidal slaughter of 800,000 people 28 years ago to colour their opinion of a country that, nowadays, plays host to a thriving farm-to-fork culinary scene.

At the despatch box on Wednesday, the Home Secretary looked stricken and bewildered at the attitude towards Rwanda's generous offer to accept a planeful of asylum seekers in return for an initial payment of just £120 million and rights to send the plane back full of its own refugees. Rwanda has an 'outstanding record' in stepping up to its international obligations, so the ECHR, the Church of England, Prince Charles, and the asylum seekers themselves would do well to examine their prejudices as they look this gift horse in the mouth. Ms. Patel wasn't calling them racists, she was leaving that for others to decide, perhaps in the reader comments below a *Daily Mail* article.

Meanwhile, Sir Keir Starmer seized the opportunity at PMQs to launch his career in stand up. Not only is the Leader of the Opposition a patriot, a royalist, a son-of-a-toolmaker, and a safe pair of hands, he is also, did you know, a bloody good laugh! All the great comics start out the same way – after excelling in academia and rising to the top of the legal profession, picking up a knighthood and establishing a happy family life, they learn from a focus group that the public finds them as engaging as an enforced fortnight at Center Parcs. Only from such personal turmoil can an artist work up material like:

'He thinks he's Obi-Wan Kenobi, the truth is, he's Jabba the Hutt!'

It takes something special to provoke a look of genuine pity in the prime minister's eyes, but Starmer's efforts succeeded where the relatives of 170,000 Covid victims fell short.

Starmer chose not to mention the previous day's aborted flight to Rwanda and went instead with the cost-of-living crisis. Fair enough, you might think, that's a real bread and butter issue and he's done well to keep his eye on the ball when the media is jumping up and down about a confected immigration row. Well, kinda, but when his spokesman was asked if Labour would reverse the Rwanda policy, he declined to answer. Did Starmer believe the policy to be morally wrong, then? Again, there was no response.

This is all rather through the looking glass. On one hand, we have Conservative ministers claiming to care about the welfare of refugees and the public perception of developing nations; on the other we have a Labour leader wrapped in the Union flag, refusing to mention a deportation policy condemned by the church and royalty. Meanwhile, we all know that, in reality:

- Priti Patel does not care at all what people think about Rwanda and would probably deport your cat if it looked at her wrong.
- Keir Starmer would reverse the policy in a heartbeat and cannot locate his Charles & Di commemorative tea set.[1]

If this seems confusing and irrelevant to affairs here in Wales, be assured that it very much is. All the participants in this charade

---

[1] This turned out to be optimistic.

have one goal, which is to win votes in the former Red Wall of Northern England, where it is assumed the next election will be won. To this end, both sides are at pains not to offend sensibilities they imagine existing in a region they know next to nothing about.[2] One thing they seem to agree on is that their target voters are a little bit racist. Not racist enough to identify as such, but gratified by being told that enjoying the spectacle of foreigners being deported is perfectly acceptable and that, in fact, it's racist *not* to support it.

The imaginary northern voter will become an omnipresent feature of politics as we approach the next election. Two variants of the species will be created by political scientists, both synthesized from pure sources of London assumption and uncontaminated by lived experience. You'll see them on party election broadcasts nodding along to Michael Gove as he promises to light an inferno of innovation in Halifax, and clinking pints matily with Wes Streeting on the set of *Emmerdale*.

So, pity the actual, flesh-and-blood northerners upon whom the current crop of aspirant statesmen will be pressing their affections in the coming months. If seduction doesn't work, you can be sure that threats will be employed – 'That's a nice levelling-up project you've got there, be a pity if something were to *happen* to it...'

If there ever comes a time when Welsh votes decide a general election, we will find out what grotesque fantasy the wider British political class has about our values and beliefs. Until then, we can only watch as they perform their strange dance for others. As far as they are concerned, we could be in Rwanda.

---

[2] 'a region about which they know next to nothing' is how this should read but I was trying to be conversational and come off like a good old pal you invite round for breakfast every Sunday so he can scream his political theories at you over the scrambled eggs.

When Scottish Eyes Are Smiling

6 February 2022

'It's a braw bricht nicht the nicht,' we all agreed as we left the Four Elms in Cardiff to return to our highland crofts after watching the day's rugby.[1] Siôn from Carmarthen had remembered a Scottish uncle and proclaimed a newfound attachment to this part of his heritage. Freddie, who's a steward at the Principality, recalled the kindness of Scottish supporters she'd encountered doing her job.

'Flower of Scotland gives me tingles,' she confided.

The Elms was selling beer in two-pint plastic glasses and I thought it wise to invest before the game so I wouldn't miss any action returning to the bar. Staring balefully into my half-finished bucket 10 minutes in, I found the answer to an eternal question: it's half-empty, definitively.

We knew something like this was coming. Last year's joy masked the gnawing suspicion that, for once, the national team had been lucky. Red cards happened at the right time, knock-ons went unnoticed, and the team had enough dog in it to ride games out to glory. Now though, with the world returning to normality, the true picture has emerged. It turns out that having poorly supported regional sides that routinely fail to challenge for titles is not irrelevant to a nation's international fortunes after all. Neither is it a given that a gifted player can switch position simply because the team is lacking a specialist.

---

[1] This came from successfully enraging my mum during the dying minutes of a Welsh defeat to Ireland when I was a kid. As she screamed tearful reproach at the telly, I went and put on a green top, announcing that I'd become an Irish supporter. No tea.

'He's done it in training and in small doses at the end of a game. We think this is a golden opportunity to answer that question,' said Wayne Pivac about his decision to gamble on Josh Adams in the centre against a side coming off a victory against the All Blacks. Well, they have their answer, and we can only hope that it didn't come at the price of Adams' confidence, nor that of Owen Watkin whose defensive abilities were disregarded.

It's true that the first half saw some questionable refereeing as Irish high tackles went unpunished. The Elms was up in arms about it whilst hope lingered, but as the second half revealed the gulf in class between the sides, talk turned to what was going wrong.

'They aren't as on it as they used to be,' said Freddie. 'After the game, they all used to be back out training on the pitch, really disciplined. All you saw in the autumn was the lawnmowers!'

As the marauding Irish slipped through tackle after tackle, people were invoking Sean Edwards, still confused as to why he was allowed to take his gifts to Paris. Whatever the trials this team are facing, it's hard to believe they would have dared return to the dressing room having missed 21 tackles were he still on the scene.

By midway through the second half the queue for the gents reached to the bar.

'Normally, that would be after the game,' sighed Jake, 'but everyone's just thought f*** it.'

Freddie and Joseph were cheerfully betting pounds on Sexton's kicks and the intensity escaped from the room to mirror the Welsh performance.

Taine Basham's interception try barely registered a cheer coming, as it did, long after there was anything left to invest in. It's not that people don't care, this was a passionate, knowledgeable crowd, but you can't expect people to risk heartbreak on a team that can't repay the stakes.

29

When the action switched to Murrayfield it was rejuvenating. Eyes were back on the screens and the amateur referees called their opinions of each phase of play. Here were two matched sides delivering for their supporters and becoming Scottish for the evening came all the easier as they turned the screw on England and held their nerve for victory. It was a sight to see. They are here next week, though, and temporary Scotsmen across Wales must steel ourselves for that and pray the team are doing the same.

The Red Scare [1]

26 June 2022

On a fateful morning in 1926, while the crowds in Merthyr chanted *'Caws a brioches'*, their leader, Wat Tyler, appeared live on Good Morning Britain from his 400,000 groat manor in Tolpuddle.

'So, are you, like, a Marxist?' demanded Richard Madeley. 'Because if you are, that means you're into revolution and bringing down capitalism!'

The studio lights flickered as, with coal stocks low, Norman Tebbit's father pedalled hard to keep the generator going.

'I'll tax you until the pips squeak!' snarled Tyler.

Hardworking families across the nation trembled at the prospect of being herded onto communal farms and *Boys from the Black Stuff* replacing *Love Island* on telly.

It's been a confusing old week for the media, hasn't it? Political commentators, who are used to speculating on how many members of the 1922 Committee can balance on the head of a pin, have been required to report on an outbreak of politics from an unthinkable source: actual working people. Their visible bewilderment at real-time industrial action has been shared by politicians of all stripes. For the Tories, it has been like Colonel Sanders pitching up to one of his restaurants and finding a chicken working behind the counter. Labour, meanwhile, had

---

[1] For reasons known only to Mark Zuckerberg, this piece went viral on Facebook and attracted thousands of readers. Mrs W and I have had to suppress memories of my behaviour that week.

expected to take a Jamie Oliver role, advocating that the chicken be killed more humanely, only to find it brandishing a meat cleaver. I mean, who do these people think they are? Politics isn't something they *do*, it's something that's done to them.

Amongst the political class, there seemed to be an inability to accept that the rail strikes were real. For them, the events could only make sense as some kind of historical cosplay, as if the Sealed Knot had turned up late to Platty Jubes and put on a re-enactment of the Battle of Orgreave.

On Sky News, Kay Burley was desperate to find out when the thuggery was scheduled to kick off. 'What are the pickets going to *do*?' she wailed as Mick Lynch amiably gestured towards four blokes in high-vis vests with placards.[2]

The RMT leader has been a headache for television news producers all week. Each deployed their most expensive presenter to skewer this interloper from another age, only to see them done up like kippers as Lynch refused to play his assigned role of angry idealogue and calmly put his case to the nation. If you require confirmation that we have not, in fact, 'returned to the 1970s' then Piers Morgan's decision to grill Lynch over whether his choice of Facebook profile photo suggested a desire to bring about global chaos should remind you we do not live in a world inhabited by Robin Day.

Meanwhile, the Prime Minister, speaking from his political heartland in Rwandashire, pointed out that some train drivers are on £70,000 a year. We can, I hope, assume he's aware that train drivers' pay has nothing to do with the current strikes and credit Johnson for using the political gambit for which he will surely be remembered: saying things that sound a bit like other things in order to confuse the public. 'Train drivers', you see, occupy the

---

[2] Lynch's effortless skewering of vapid news presenters ought to have demonstrated that the public is thirsty for politicians who calmly state a reasoned case. That said, you need a reasoned case to state.

same space in our mental filing cabinets as 'rail workers'. Likewise, who amongst us has time to clearly label 'European Court of Human Rights' so that we don't confuse it with 'European Court of Justice'? Remoaners, that's who, say no more.

And where was the King of the Remoaners as anarcho-syndicalism became this week's ice bucket challenge? When the world's most cautious baby emerged quietly from the womb in 1962, he could have done without being named after the firebrand founder of the Labour Party, Keir Hardie. Historical Keirs had it easy, anyone can swan about with a hipster beard representing a uniform demographic against a cigar-chomping ruling class that hasn't had any media training. Your modern Keir must address the concerns of his traditional base without demonising aspirational values so he can build a broad coalition around progressive ideas that serve the needs of a modern economy whilst ensuring that workers are fully protected against...hello? Is anybody listening? Come back from that picket line and discuss this reasonably!

As I was stuck in traffic on the A470 on Tuesday, I listened to interviews with the RMT representatives and with those from Network Rail. It struck me how, between the actual protagonists, there seemed to be a great deal of mutual respect. This was no rancorous clash of ideologies; it was a simple dispute between interested parties that had come to a head. The contrast was not between those involved but with commentators and politicians who are so divorced from the working life of the country that they can only discuss it as a mythological battleground upon which ghosts from the past can be invoked to spook the populace one way or another.

* *Wat Tyler's spokesman explained he was unavailable for comment, having been at a work event with Richard II for the duration of the Glastonbury Festival.*

Rivers of Wales

26 May 2022

Nothing's solid here; all's sketched and coloured in shifting tones of water and light. Even history has become ambiguous, uncertain. These are drowned lands, their legends tide-steeped, wind-honed.

Jim Perrin is known, primarily, as a mountain writer. His collections on Yr Wyddfa and the hills of Wales, to which this book could be considered a companion, sit alongside his biographies of climbers – Whillans, Menlove, Shipton and Tilman – as meditations on the desire to negotiate with the implacable. In his grief memoir, *West,* we encounter him lashed to the Old Man of Hoy, reckoning with devastating loss, and finding an ally in the rock as he ascends.

Where a mountain might offer rigorous certainty against the confusion of existence, a river reveals us on our course, acting as a vital correlation to the wisdom of our choices. It is reactive to humanity, a living scorecard of our ecological performance and, in *Rivers of Wales*[1] Perrin frames environmental catastrophe within a wider picture of moral decline brought about by the political direction of the UK over the last half century.

This is not, however, a political tract, but a deeply personal exposition of the physical, cultural, and historical riches that our rivers offer. We are taken by the hand along their banks as Perrin recounts folklore, reminiscence and historical context set against precise, descriptive writing that evidences the author's deep immersion in these landscapes.

---

[1] Jim Perrin's *Rivers of Wales* (2022) is available from: carreg-gwalch.cymru

Perrin is at pains to contextualise his work within a tradition of nature writing by exponents whose subject was a way of life, rather than an aspect of it. We are gifted loving introductions to Borrow, Kilvert, Gibbings, and Condry alongside arch dismissals of Wordsworth, whom one can envisage sipping a soy latte above Tintern Abbey in unsuitable shoes, and those contemporary nature writers whose impressions of landscape serve metropolitan preoccupations.

This is writing from *within* the landscape. We feel a depth of connection between author and subject that speaks of a symbiosis that has evolved over a lifetime. There is a passage in the chapter on Afon Teifi where we find Perrin fretting over the fate of a solitary cygnet, whose precarious tenure in our world comes to stand for all that we are at risk to lose. Invoking the loss of his son, Perrin brings wretched experience to bear in a plea to have us *feel* what is at stake if our natural habitats are sacrificed to commercial vandalism. Here, history, politics, aesthetics, and memoir dissolve into the polluted waters of the Teifi, and we are left on its banks to decide our parts in its future wellbeing.

Along the way, we are well-served for entertainment, with ripe anecdotes, Sebald-esque digressions, and catty swipes at those who are too well-insulated to feel them. If, for instance, you become weighed down with an explanation of Pelagian theology, the author's cat pops up to proffer its opinion and usher you through to less demanding terrain. A gentle self-mockery flavours the narrative and allows latitude for Perrin's more acerbic observations.

For all that this is an opinionated book, it does not seek to persuade. Perrin's views are set atop his scholarship and experience for the reader to evaluate. He recalls characters he met who lived authentically in these landscapes, describing the effect that the rhythms of nature had upon their humanity, and how this mode of being is seemingly lost to us. There is a feeling that the author's own lifestyle, born of the post-war consensus, has been fenced out of viability by the commercialisation of the countryside. Where once a living could be made instructing urban children about the natural world, now the market privileges shooting parties for those so inclined who can afford them. Pained regret at this direction of travel infuses these pages as Perrin, unlashed from the rockface, heads towards the estuary with dwindling company. Tag along is my advice; you're bound to learn something.

Empty Leaders of Imaginary Voters

31 July 2022

There are a great many things at which I am absolutely useless.[1] If I manage to perform a task like, say, changing a lightbulb, Mrs W smiles indulgently at me as one might at a toddler who has tied his shoelaces for the first time. For the most part, however, I am discouraged by all around me from interfering in areas of life where I have no business. Consequently, I've had a lot of experience in dealing with professional tradespeople across the vast array of disciplines that are beyond my mastery.

I've found that it's wise to be cheerfully open about my own utter ignorance when in the company of someone who knows what they are talking about.

'So, *that's* how you open the bonnet, I've always been afraid to ask,' seems to go down far better with Johnny Expert than,

'Obviously, I've tried flushing the alternator with WD40 but I'm not familiar with the rivet alignment on the Mark 3, which is why I've had to call you.'

The latter approach betrays a psychological tic that can befall the unwary in middle age: a reluctance to believe that one is less than adequate in any area. Working for people like this must be a nightmare. Not only do you have to do the job, but also pretend that the client's grasp of the situation is on a level with your own.

Of course, the middle-aged know-all is guaranteed to be at the polling station by 6.55 a.m. every single election, so dealing with this lot is the stock in trade of politicians the world over. Where plumbers and mechanics have the advantage over

---

[1] Just don't. I'm way ahead of you.

candidates is that there is always another customer round the corner. Politicians have one shot every five years to create a good impression and they must make it with people who will reliably vote. This is why we see them painfully trying to second-guess the values of people they would cross the street to avoid under normal circumstances.

At this week's hustings in Leeds, Ready4Rishi opted to open with a 'Brown person with a suntan' joke that could have been from a 1976 edition of *The Comedians*. It's hard to know what to be offended at first about that. The scenarios I can identify are these:

Ready4Rishi just assumes his own party members like a bit of race-based humour and couldn't care less about it.

The Tory Party membership is *so* racist that he's been told his only chance of winning favour is by joining in.

Those involved believe racial sensitivity to be redundant since Alesha Dixon won *Strictly*, so we should all chillax and take a joke.

Awkwardly, the audio suggested that the gag was received in silence other than by two guffawing men whose nephews are already dreading Christmas. Whatever assumptions the speechwriters were operating under seem to have been wide of the mark. You see, much as some of us might prefer the mechanic to nod along respectfully to our misdiagnosis of a fault in the spherical flange, we're not nuts enough to demand they act on it rather than actually fixing the problem.

It would be reassuring to think that politicians made policy from a combination of personal conviction and expertise. Appealing to us by pretending to be as thick as they assume us to be used to be the preserve of tabloid editors; now it is so embedded in political practice that appointing Nadine Dorries to the cabinet merely lent authenticity to the crass banality our leaders think they should embody.

Which brings me to Keir Starmer.

Sirkieth the Cautious arrives to fix your car in a set of overalls, but is so worried about upsetting you that he pronounces it good for another 100,000 miles and sacks anybody who points out that all that's left of it is a clown holding a steering wheel.

Reading the moment is a core skill in politics, and if you lead a party called 'Labour' which everyone knows was founded by the trade unions, then refusing to pick a side when the entire nation is being offered pay cuts after 12 years of austerity is a baffling decision. Sirkieth's imaginary voter looks at a payslip that doesn't cover the gas bill and sighs,

'Thank God I can't go to the pub this weekend. Sirkieth's dogmatic adherence to Treasury principles has helped me to play my part in stabilising the economy.'

This mythical working man wakes up every morning terrified that Red Robbo[2] has risen from the dead to resume a demarcation dispute from 1978.

Historically, politicians didn't care at all what we thought. On one side you had the raw power of the Establishment threatening you with penury or worse; on the other, bright, self-educated plebs brandishing clever ideas from books they'd read. T'internet has fooled us all into thinking we have agency, and our politicians now offer absolutely nothing other than what they have been told we think ourselves. We have leaders whose followers are figments of their imagination. Best go on a car maintenance course.

---

[2] My West Midlands origins on display here. Derek Robinson was Best Man at my mate's parents' wedding. They were apolitical and apparently he was an absolute gent.

Time for Tubby Bye-Byes

5 February 2023

It's always gratifying when geopolitical events bear out what you have been saying for years, so I felt supremely validated on Thursday when the Chinese government sent a powerful visual message suggesting that the United States of America was, in reality, a 246-years-long episode of *Teletubbies*.

Whilst simple American folk gazed up at a large, spherical object[1] that signified their infantile status in the sweep of global history, China twisted the knife.

'The airship is from China and is civilian in nature, used for meteorological and other scientific research. Due to the influence of westerly winds and its limited control capability, the airship deviated from its intended course,' smirked the Chinese Foreign Ministry.

It seems that those of us who assumed a rather dour aspect to the workings of the Chinese Communist Party had failed to discern its mastery of dry humour. Once you're tuned into it, however, you can't fail to titter at their top bants. Sending a harmless object to hover over the most paranoid nation on earth is a wind-up of the first order.

Remember, Orson Welles' 1938 radio dramatisation of *War of the Worlds* managed to convince many of his skittish countrymen that heat-ray wielding Martians had arrived in

---

[1] A large, unexplained balloon, believed to be of Chinese origin, had appeared in the sky over the western USA. *Nation.Cymru*'s weekend editor Sarah Morgan Jones created an image of Xi Jinping's face superimposed on to the *Teletubbies* sun for this article and I encourage you to seek it out.

Grover's Mill, New Jersey. But that's so long ago, you might argue. America has come a long way since then, you'd think, wouldn't you? However, whilst Xi Jinping's ball of mirth was hanging over Montana, the Congress was hosting a furious debate over whether Georgia Representative Marjorie Taylor Greene had blamed the outbreak of Californian wildfires on 'Jewish space lasers'.

American paranoia is what lies behind the tiresome boastfulness that characterises the nation's public face to the world. The 'shining city on the hill' can only outrun the demands of its collective conscience by generating revolving external threats that serve to distract from its misdeeds. The British are going to get us! The French! The Germans! The Russians! The Arabs! Somewhere, buried beneath the 'greatest nation on earth' razzmatazz, lies the nagging knowledge that the country's behaviour is grossly at odds with the ideals of its constitution. On some level we can all empathise, we might have forgotten an aged aunt's birthday for the third year running, misgendered our eldest child's emotional-support stick insect, or reneged on a series of legally binding treaties with the rightful owners of the land upon which we brutalise our slaves, but we're the good guys, right? Also, balloons spook us, so just knock it off.

Americans, though, like Andrew 'Righty Tighty' Davies, are too obvious a target for mockery. We would be better occupied worrying about our own egregious history of colonial misconduct. Beyond our victimhood at the hands of hedge fund managers, coal owners, Norman conquerors, Roman invaders, Maggie Thatcher, and every submerged village that ever poked its steeple through a drought is the money we are living on. Whether it's flowing through share dividends or Universal Credit payments every penny derives part of its value from the opium Britain took from India and forced on China. We have long memories in this disadvantaged corner of the empire: *Cofiwch Dryweryn* and every other foul degradation that the Empire visited on Cymru. Remember also that we are lumped in as protagonists whether we

41

like it or not. If a balloon appears over Tregaron in the future, knowing your daps from your trainers might not exempt you from scrutiny.

The Knives Are Out

17 July 2022

There's nothing like naked ambition to reveal the inner child in a person. Dangle anyone's deepest desire in front of them and you'll see the raw fundamentals that drive their personality: the stuff that therapists are there for. None of us looks at our best when we are grasping for something, and we are normal human beings, so when the emotional cripples who people parliament compete for the mother lode of validation they believe to exist in 10 Downing Street, it can resemble the dog-end of a sixth birthday party that's featured too many E-numbers.

We rarely see the little darlings unsupervised. Ministers are usually dressed for school by their departmental civil servants who have reminded them to be polite before dropping them off in the morning. During a leadership election, grown-ups are banished and there is nobody to check the contestants' homework before they hand it in. As any teacher will confirm, you only really see what they are like on a school trip.

So, what do we have on our hands?

Ready4Rishi has been Head Boy his entire life. At conception, one imagines his father's most responsible sperm approaching the egg with a fully costed plan for Sunak Minor's education – to include a budgetary allowance for on-point leisurewear. What an absolute ballache he must have been for Boris Johnson, urging caution three times before breakfast and refusing to join in with the bullying. His problem is that he looks so destined to be PM that it's irresistible to spoil it for him. If I were a Tory backbencher, I'd introduce him to smoking.

Something's going on around Penny Mordaunt that we haven't been let in on. On face value she's a Tory backbencher's dream: youngish, well-spoken with a military background, and reputedly possessed of a barrack room sense of humour, you'd think she ticked every possible box. Someone with Establishment poke, however, clearly disagrees and this morning's *Mail on Sunday* devotes six articles to trashing her, whilst Lord Frost, the *éminence puce* of Brexit, has been rushing around TV studios to insist she's a wrong 'un. Ms. Mordaunt, it seems, has untold history.

Kemi Badenoch, meanwhile, is strictly about the future. With no chance of winning this time, she's free to burnish her reputation without immediate consequence. Tellingly, she was the candidate willing to stick the boot directly into Mordaunt during the first televised debate by invoking the trans issue, with its vast, deranged hinterland of woke phobia. Earlier in the day on LBC she had dismissed criticism from comedian Dane Baptiste by announcing, 'I don't need people whose only experience of being black is being an ethnic minority in the UK to tell me what that means.' With Michael Gove in her corner, it's fair to assume we'll be hearing a great deal from Kemi Badenoch over the coming years.

Tom Tugendhat, it turns out, used to be a Super Army Soldier. Did you know that? Because he was an actual soldier in a proper war and he's pretty disgusted at what he's found since lowering himself into the fetid swamp of politics. If horned-rimmed rectitude is your thing, then Tom has a pleasing 1930s vibe about him but he's a bit John Major for a party still gnawing on the red meat of Brexit and will be left to chunter away about decency until he jacks it in and starts writing books on military history.

Which leaves Liz Truss. Putting the sensational weirdness of Liz into words has been taxing writers for a while. She's an authentic jolt to the senses when she goes full *League of Gentlemen*. Blinking furiously, her thoughts seem to collide behind her eyes on the way to finding expression in a series of disconnected statements and unsettling facial expressions.

Dressing up as Margaret Thatcher is something most of us do at one time or another, but exactly replicating a specific 1979 outfit for a TV debate is a step beyond harmless fun.

One of these characters will soon have won life on the terms they set out as children. Events will conspire to suggest that, just as they suspected, they *are* special and marked out for greatness. Our role in all this is to ensure they hate every moment of it.

Lib-Dem to PM

24 Jul 2022

For all the doom and gloomsters out there, we had some fabulous economic news this week. Last month's figures show that, thanks to Platty Jubes, sales in the food sector were up a whopping three per cent. Granted, this was almost entirely accounted for by alcohol, but I think we can confidently chalk this up as a Brexit benefit. Only since throwing off the shackles of the EU have we, as a nation, felt able to express our unanimous love and support for the Royal Family by skulling crates of Stella in the hot tub. In republican France, for instance, a four-day public holiday can only be granted by the town's Chief Bureaucrat if it has been signed off in a plenary session of the European Parliament. Surely, Nigel Farage is due a peerage from Her Maj in recognition of his services to patriotic binge drinking if nothing else.

Liz Truss, of course, led the way in our national celebrations. South-West Norfolk was reportedly drunk dry of Jaegermeister as the Foreign Secretary took on all-comers in a three-day game of Fuzzy Duck before challenging Brexit hardman Steve Baker to arm wrestle for the rights to conduct the ceremonial vomiting of the camembert.

Liz, you see, has 'been on a journey'. Having grown up in a socialist household, weeping as her pleas for small, individual packs of cereal were ignored in favour of a communal box of Frosties, she initially broke from tyranny by joining the Liberal Democrats. As a student, she spoke at a conference calling for the abolition of the monarchy, a decision she apparently regretted 'almost immediately'. I'd like to stick up for her on that one. It's hard to think of any entanglement with the Lib Dems that doesn't result in lifelong regret; their heady cocktail of besandled centrism and moral superiority has banjaxed everyone from Shirley Williams to John Cleese. Just say no, kids. Liberal Demness comes in many shades of piss-weak yellow, though, and it's a bit puzzling that our Maggie-channelling Foreign Sec. chose the one that includes snatching the sparkly hat from her royal namesake's head.

Once ensconced in the bosom of the Conservative Party, Liz found common cause with the fellow Europeans that she met there and campaigned for Remain. There's an easy logic to that trajectory: ditch the perpetual losers and latch on to the similar wing of a party that knows how to win elections. That wing, however, has been mangled beyond repair by the rotary blades of Brexit, leaving the party to circle endlessly in pursuit of its own ideological rectum.

Liz's transformation into an ardent Brexiteer isn't particularly surprising. Ambitious politicians always view principles as window dressing. The confusing element is that the true believers seem to have embraced her so unquestioningly. It started with Jacob Rees-Mogg and Naddy D endorsing her as a stronger Brexiteer than even themselves. The two statespeople opted to issue this address outside Number 10, thus confirming rumours that Liz was Johnson's favoured successor. There's a lot to unpick here, not least that Johnson's own Brexit bona fides are as flimsy as Nadine's novels.[1] Primarily, though, we have to question why a Remain voter would appeal to these two more than Rishi Sunak, who was writing about leaving the EU whilst still a hugely popular and stylishly turned-out schoolboy.

And they weren't alone. By the end of last week, she had received backing from the Ian Paisley of Euroscepticism, Steve Baker, who explained that Liz's 'journey' was one that 'the whole

---

[1] Obviously, I read one to ensure I was being even-handed. *Nobility Thwarted*, I think it was called.

47

nation needed to take.' This suggests that the ERG intends to reach out to stubborn Remainers by offering up Liz as a lost sheep who has seen the light and turned to the path of righteousness. Well, OK, but I don't remember them giving a kipper's fundament for the opinions of Remainers before, and her presentational style is, shall we say, suboptimal, so what is going on?

Liz, against all economic precedent and advice, has agreed to cut corporation tax and to do it right now. The high priests of Brexit, who have sold their project to the nation as a patriotic religion, are prepared to back a Remain-voting, former republican Liberal Democrat who stands next to no chance of winning a general election so that share prices will inflate and those with skin in the game can cash out.

When the winter bites, and gas prices surge, expect to be reminded of the Blitz whilst you burn some sovereignty to keep warm.

Dead Man's Corner

13 Feb 2022

The Wetherspoons on Cardiff's City Road, in an act of conspicuous cultural sensitivity, was offering a special of haggis, neeps and tatties as Scottish supporters began to arrive on Thursday night. Well, it's what they like, isn't it?

What they very much don't like is the effect on a rugby team that Dan Biggar can have when he feels that it isn't operating at the level he demands. Yesterday's victory was led from the front and, it is safe to assume, built upon a week's leadership in training that reflected Biggar's personal standards. After last week's debacle in Dublin, his 100th cap was going one of two ways but, dragging a knee injury sustained early on, he seemed to infuse his team with the will to endure all that Scotland could throw at them.

Having misunderstood the news and being under the impression that 130,000 Russian troops were advancing westwards from Sebastopol near Pontypool, Mrs W and I fled Cardiff and watched the game from the relative safety of Cardigan RFC. Arriving early, we were soon joined at our table by the genial triumvirate of Eric, Hayden and Denzil: gentlemen of sufficient seniority to have been present when Delme and the boys beat the All Blacks at Stradey Park in 1972.

'There used to be eight of us sat here,' Eric recalled. 'You're sitting in Dead Man's Corner...'[1]

And in the lead up to the game, it did feel distinctly funereal.

---

[1] Cardigan is an absolute gem of a rugby club. I felt slightly guilty for diluting its perfect atmosphere with my presence.

Denzil was only here because the club's no-swearing rule guaranteed better prospects for his eternal soul than had he been watching at home. I don't know about you, but Scotland is always a nervy game for me. Ireland is the litmus test: objectively they are our equals so that one can go either way every year. France are, to put it delicately, unpredictable: the right decor in the changing rooms might cause them to defeat the All Blacks having lost to Tonga the week before. Why bookies offer odds on them is a mystery. The England game has nothing to do with sport at all, at least for us, and occupies the emotional space generally taken up by births and deaths. A loss to Scotland, however, usually means that we will be scrapping it out for the wooden spoon. In days gone by, before Carwyn James sprinkled his genius over Italy, it meant worse than that. This Scotland side were looking to build on back-to-back Calcutta Cup victories and supplant Wales in the European pecking order properly.

14-14 at half-time.

'Don't fill up on nuts,' Eric advised, 'they're bringing out free sausages and chips!'

Behind the bar there are beautifully preserved jerseys displayed. The barman caught me admiring Brynmor Williams' Cardiff RFC centenary shirt.

'He's my uncle, used to play here.'

'I played hooker with him,' the fellow next to me confirmed.

'Funny thing, he never captained *this* club, his brother did though.'

'Right enough.'

Hope remained in short supply as the second half kicked off.

'We're having a great afternoon, if we lose, we lose,' the triumvirate agreed.

And when Scotland posted the first points of the second half, that prospect seemed all too likely. But this wasn't the Wales of

50

last week.

'Where's the intensity?' Biggar had implored the team in Dublin. Today, they had rediscovered it, and no breakdown was conceded without a fight. With the crowd in full voice, almighty scraps for the ball took place around the halfway line as the closely matched sides tucked into the meat of the game.

'Ireland are a class above, that's what we're learning here,' warned Hayden, lugubriously, but you can only play who's in front of you and as the half played out, it became clear that Wales weren't going to fold this time. Finally, the Scots began to give a little, and Wales were able to mount a sustained attack on their line with 10 minutes left. With a penalty already awarded, Biggar opted to drop a goal, rather than take a place kick or press for the line. It seemed a strange decision, we were puzzled by it in Cardigan. The next ten minutes proved him right. The captain had handed Scotland the ball and invited them to attack Wales' three-point lead. In doing so, he placed faith in a team that had been written off and derided all week, giving them the opportunity to redeem themselves. At 78 minutes, with a penalty awarded, Biggar's limp had worsened to the point he was substituted. Tellingly, he refused to leave the field until he'd found touch. From the side-lines, he had to watch Wales defend 10 phases of play with 80 minutes up. He'd shown them what they were about, though and he wasn't disappointed.

We've seen prettier Welsh victories, but this one held genuine significance. What looked last week like the inevitable consequence of a failing system, was reversed by the determination of a team that wouldn't accept that narrative.

The triumvirate looked 10 years younger as we left Dead Man's Corner.

The Road to Tunbridge Wells

7 Aug 2023

Andrew Bailey, Governor of the Bank of England, doesn't know precisely how much he is paid[1] but it's sufficient for him to forgo the 1.5% rise he was offered this year. From this lofty vantage point, he felt confident this week in alerting unionised workers to the moral case against demanding salaries that keep pace with inflation.

'In this world it is the people who are least well-off who are worst affected because they don't have the bargaining power,' he said. Let's unpack this a little, shall we? The governor is responsible for keeping inflation under control and appointed to do so by the government. Now, with inflation heading for 13%, he wants workers with rights to feel ashamed of disadvantaging citizens who have no rights because the government who appointed him refuses to give them any.

This is the 'So having a public library is more important to you than funding a cancer ward, is it?' line of extortion that worked so well for Osborne & Co. during austerity. The key to its success lies in persuading people to ignore the vast profits that are made during a crisis and demanding that the mass of people forego their Costa coffees for the greater good. We are encouraged to believe that the economy is a living organism that is suffering an illness. Only by sacrifice can we play our parts in willing the creature back to health, so that it can resume laying golden eggs for us all to share. Oddly, however, the more stricken it is, the more eggs it seems able to lay for those with the means to buy up the assets we have to sell off cheaply to pay for its

---

[1] He'd been asked in an interview.

recovery.

Austerity, of course, was pronounced over by Sajid Javid in September 2019. But for the pandemic, we'd all be down the local Tesla dealership this weekend ordering new sets of rims. If it hadn't been for that pesky virus, Boris would have levelled us up good and proper, as is the heart's desire of every true Tory. Except, it seems, Ready4Rishi. There were two pieces of compelling footage released from Planet Tory this week. In one, Boris Johnson was shown galumphing around the dancefloor at his wedding party like a tasered bear, while the other had Ready4Rishi exposing levelling up as the mendacious bollocks it always was. As wealthy codgers sweltered under trees in an agreeable Tunbridge Wells garden, Ready4Rishi courted their votes by boasting that he'd diverted funds from deprived inner cities to deserving communities such as their own.

'Red Wall' voters had already been thrown under the bus by Liz Truss this week with her short-lived policy of cutting the wages of civil servants depending on how impoverished the godawful northern hole she'd relocated them to remained under her governance. And this is how they treat *England*.

The *I'm a Diagnosed Narcissist... Get Me Out of Here* roadshow pulled into Cardiff this week for the Tory hustings. 48 hours earlier Truss had described Nicola Sturgeon as an 'attention seeker' who was 'best ignored'. Neither candidate actually wore a pith helmet as they garbled a bit of Welsh or giggled about Shirley Bassey and sheep, but the tone was of an address to the natives, including admiration for the 'vision' of Andrew RT Davies, of whom, I suspect, neither had heard until being prepped for the event.[2]

The substance, such as it was, promised 'activism' from Westminster to counterbalance the powers of the Senedd. This prospect was eagerly received by an audience whom Ready4Rishi

---

[2] He's real, I promise you. Google him.

had treated to a warm-up show from promising Llanelli goth performer, Michael Howard. Clutching their 'Ready4Rish!' and 'Liz for Leader!' cards, they seemed a socially awkward bunch, perhaps more used to practicing their politics alone. One issue cohered them above all others: the M4 relief road. Both candidates promised this to wild applause by these tormented souls who see redemption on the road to Tunbridge Wells.

After this contest is over, the party will stop talking to itself and, once again, address us as if we have a common purpose. The client media will explain that we are all in the same crisis and must tighten our belts until it passes. But we're not, are we? You've seen their lips moving and saying so. In Tunbridge Wells they know the score and are preparing to snap up cheap assets as we speak. They have a government that acts on their behalf whatever the circumstances. The majority of the UK has no such thing.

Brown to the Rescue?

14 Aug 2022

Do you fancy having a bash at running the country? I only ask because none of the people supposedly in with a shot at doing so seem to have the remotest interest. Obviously, we have the corpse of Boris attending to matters of state with characteristically selfless devotion to public service, but you would think his potential successors would be champing at the bit to impose their political vision on our beleaguered nation; cometh the hour, cometh the... Oh my God, is that Gordon Brown? He's still sentient? I'd assumed he'd be imposing a fiscal rule on the bingo sessions in a Kirkaldy home for the bewildered by now.

But no, as we stare down the barrels of utter financial ruin, the brooding son of the manse has emerged as the only politico with a plan to address the forthcoming hike in the energy cap. Here's the plan:

Don't have a hike in the energy cap.

Now, I don't know about you, but I find the clarity of purpose in this plan rather attractive. 'B...b...but, who will pay for all the expensive gas and leccy?' demanded the nodding dogs that comprise the broadcast media. Here's where 'Mr Fiscal Responsibility' went rogue. It turns out that we can, I'm almost afraid to say this out loud, force the energy companies and their shareholders to pay for our grannies not freezing to death. And, criminy, if the energy companies go bust we can (foreboding music)... nationalise them.

Now, I know this might come as a shock. For forty years, including those when Mr Brown was in government, we have filed to the ballot box murmuring the sacred mantra: 'Private legs good; public legs bad.' But apparently, back in the mists of time, before Richard Branson had supplanted Hippocrates as a healthcare influencer, there used to be a quaint tradition whereby matters of life and death for the public were decided by elected representatives rather than board meetings. It might be a little late in the day for Mr Brown to be coming on like Nye Bevan, but at least he's having a go, isn't he?

And that's more than can be said of any other relevant political voices at the moment.

Where, you might wonder, is Michael Gove? He's not given to long periods of polite silence, is he? Similarly, when was the last time you went so long without the sweet music of Jess Phillips' profound utterances on national life? Cat got your tongue, Bab?[1]

Paging Nigel Farage... Mr Farage, can you hear us here in the country you love so dearly? Sorry to interrupt when you are so deeply ensconced in Donald Trump's fundament, but the post-Brexit masses are in dire need of a dose of sovereignty in their pay-as-you-go meters, any ideas? No?

John McDonnell spent 10 years producing alternative budgets to chivvy up Gordon Brown. Now is your moment, John! You are freed from the admittedly demanding role of lending intellectual ballast to Jeremy Corbyn, so speak up.

Even the king of unwelcome advice, Tony Blair, seems absent from the fray. With the regularity of a wooden bird in a Swiss clock, he emerges to instruct us all, in that peculiar, peevish manner he has developed, to conform to his particular brand of common sense. Convinced of his normality, he generally can't restrain himself from appearing on TV to order us all to become

---

[1] Her performative Brummieness sends me into conniptions. Like me, she went to a very nice school in Birmingham, and you do not emerge from those sounding as if you're selling knock-off vapes in the Bull Ring. Fraud, fraud, fraud.

poorer or go to war with somewhere we've barely heard of. He's sitting this one out, though. Doesn't want to impose.

Which leaves us with the three characters who actually hold some influence.

Sirkieth has been having a good think and will release his fully costed plan on Monday. He's trailed this with a proposal for pre-payment meters which will save people £46 per year. My suspicion is that Brown's intervention will force the under-seasoned tin of luncheon meat to embolden whatever he had planned, but his predisposition seems to veer from caution to cowardice, so don't expect too much.

Ready4Rishi might actually throw you a few quid. He's had a good shake of the Magic Money Tree during Covid and is so blithely unaware of consequence that he's constructing a £400k swimming pool at home and hang what anyone says. Threaten him with a payment strike and he'll pay your bills in a heartbeat.

But it's the surgical appliance to whom we must look in reality. For Liz, proud Yorkshirewoman and pork marketeer, any direct help for you as a consumer of private energy companies is a 'handout'. If you are a little colder this winter, you should be warmed by the knowledge that profits won't be jeopardised on her watch. Only they will. Because when this pantomime leadership contest is over and a chill is in the air, she'll no longer be beholden to Conservative members but to you and me. I don't know about you, but I get a bit testy if I'm cold for prolonged periods of time and my mood isn't generally soothed by lectures on Thatcherite doctrine. I'll bet you my hot water bottle that, eventually, Gordon Brown's solution will be adopted.[2]

---

[2] Was it? I don't even know any more. The bills come in for seemingly random amounts and I tot up if I've got enough for a Chinese on Friday before carrying on blankly with my day. Privilege? Yes, but a dispiriting version.

A Chill Sets In

21 Aug 2022

The nights are drawing in, aren't they? Soon be Christmas and we can all look forward to toasting a single chestnut on the space heater we've huddled around to watch the Queen's speech. Perhaps she'll wear fingerless gloves to show solidarity with her subjects; visible breath would be a bonus. As Dad carves the pigeon, we'll get out photographs of Christmases past and explain to the children that, in the olden days, we used to put on Christmas jumpers *ironically*, rather than to protect against hypothermic organ failure during *Eastenders*.

So, things being what they are, if I were called 'Lord Frost' I'd think about adopting a low profile. If there's anyone people don't need to hear from at the moment, it's a Brexit-smeared escapee from Narnia.

But here he is, looking like the fat one in *Dalziel & Pascoe*, with his latest pronouncement. A couple of weeks ago he blithely dismissed wind turbines as 'medieval technology' that are unnecessary as we're not in a climate emergency. Now, he's brought his omniscience to bear on constitutional matters, telling Wales and Scotland that we have mistaken ourselves for nations and that all talk of independence needs to be legislated out of the conversation.

Frost's prominence signals a cultural shift. For years we have been subject to governance by the *Daily Mail*. Spiteful xenophobia cloaking the theft of assets by the wealthy has become as familiar as Ant & Dec in the UK: death, taxes, and Richard Littlejohn.

Frost, though, is the darling of the *Daily Express*. While the

Mail offers its readers a fix of nastiness to shore up their prejudices and usher them into the voting booth, the *Express* deals in pure fantasy that is designed to stimulate the thin dreaming of English care home residents for whom each day is the same as, yet slightly worse than, the last. For them, Frost is the patriotic knight who rode to the rescue of Brexit after the cowardly retreat of Theresa May. He is the true believer in whom people who believe themselves to have been betrayed by everyone from Tony Blair to Jimmy Savile can trust.

Only they can't. In 2015, the gammon's gammon was heading up the Scotch Whisky Association, in which role he argued, *at the Scottish Parliament,* that the UK should remain in the EU. He followed this up by writing an article warning of the catastrophe awaiting Britain if it left the Single Market. After leading the botched negotiations with Brussels under Johnson, he now advocates abandoning the very agreement he signed. Like Liz Truss, his Brexit bona fides are a pose at best. But it is in terms of Brexit that Frosty the Showman casts his attack upon devolution. His fear that devolution risks 'mission creep' towards independence is not based on any cultural attachment to Wales or Scotland. Rather, he sees our loss from the UK as a visible humiliation before the EU. Like every inadequate abuser, he doesn't want his victim, but is terrified that someone else might.

It's a truism that independence campaigns flourish if they can assert the cultural case above the economic argument. Tory Party chaos seems to be turning this on its head. Frost makes the cultural case better than Adam Price or Nicola Sturgeon could dream of. It used to be that claiming the UK suppressed the self-determination of its constituent nations was a fringe position. Now, with charlatans such as Frost courting Express readers for Liz Truss, the UK is out and proud about telling us to shut up and do as we are told.

Meanwhile, the economic argument around independence has shifted from lofty questions about the viability of a new currency to whether or not the Westminster government is willing to allow people to freeze to death in their own homes. Brexit allowed all our arguments to be carried out on an abstract plane. Widening inequality and crumbling public services have been kept from people's thoughts by endless parlour games involving the notion of 'sovereignty' and, when that wore thin, 'woke culture'.

In the coming months, this charade will come to an abrupt halt. Politicians who have made careers from stoking xenophobia and fabricating threats from anyone trying to stem the civic decline of the UK are going to run into a wall of desperate need amongst the people they have misled.

So, when fake-Brexiteer Lord Frost is Foreign Secretary under fellow fake-Brexiteer, Liz Truss, they are quickly going to run out of external threats to blame for the financial ruin that we are facing. It seems to me that casting Wales and Scotland as the enemy within is the penultimate bullet in their gun before turning it on themselves.[1]

---

[1] I underestimated the willingness of sailors on the good ship Tory to throw each other overboard.

Boomergeddon

4 Sept 2022

It has become perversely fashionable to heap opprobrium upon the Baby Boomer generation. Millennials carp about rental costs, GenZ seem to think they have a God-given right to a functioning ecosystem, and the ingrates of Generation X persist in complaining about the Boomer-led innovation of television-based parenting. The remaining members of the WW2 generation are probably joining in too, but they've been put into homes, so we can't hear them.

'Twas ever thus for this misunderstood generation. Their spiritual leader, Roger Daltry, was so maligned in his 20s that he hoped he'd die before he got old. He didn't though, opting instead to open a trout farm and appear in a string of American Express adverts before becoming a leading cheerleader for Brexit. The EU, Roger explained, was 'too divorced from ordinary people'.

Brexit is, of course, only one of the political masterstrokes that have been made possible by the largest generational voting block in history. In the 1960s, newly enfranchised members of the Beat Generation celebrated their first decade of hegemony over national life by voting to abolish university tuition fees. In the 1970s, workplace rights occupied centre stage, only to be replaced in the 1980s by a focus on enabling the purchase of property. Cynics have suggested that the tendency of Boomers to vote for the reversal of all of the above once it no longer benefited them speaks of a certain self-interested aspect to their politics. Whilst it's true that the triple lock on pensions became an election-deciding policy as they entered retirement, let's not forget that without Boomer votes we wouldn't have had Sure Start centres, until they voted to close them down again.

Boomer influence has been startlingly evident during the Tory leadership hustings, which have often resembled rainy-day entertainment on a Saga boutique cruise. Scapegoat Bingo involves the contestants making the most horrified face they can muster when presented with the ills of contemporary society before ascribing them to one of two culprits: Sadiq Khan or The Woke. I shan't speculate on why mention of the Mayor of London provokes howling fury amongst this audience, previously preoccupied with their 'legitimate concerns about immigration', but it's safe to say that he's out of the running for a presenting gig on Countdown.

Sadiq Khan does, at least, exist. The Woke, on the other hand, are a nebulous presence, rather like the Borg in *Star Trek*. You are unaware of their existence until you've read about a fireman being sent for diversity training. Ask Alexa to 'show me cultural appropriation' and she will play you clips of Julia Hartley-Brewer ascribing wokeness to everything from Covid vaccines to Gary Lineker. The bleak irony here is that its original usage was in African-American culture to denote alertness to racist practices like, er, thieving culturally specific phrases.

There will be a special place in hell for Generation X collaborators like Hateley-Spewer and Dan Wootton. These are people young enough to have fully understood why Kurt Cobain couldn't take it anymore, yet they shill for the vested interests that usher their parents into ever more ludicrous political positions to explain away the chaos we are now all enduring at the end of forty years of fantasy economics.

There is much to be said about democracy in an ageing society. Our primary crucible for forming political opinions is the workplace. Here, we see up-to-date evidence of how society is actually functioning and, whatever our roles, filter this through lived experience and professional expertise. The further into retirement we go, the more distant this reality becomes, leaving us prey to the machinations of newspaper proprietors and online lunatics.

While the picture on the ground becomes ever more worrying, our politicians have distracted enough of the electorate with threats of cultural annihilation that nothing useful is now being done. As the NHS struggles and inflation makes paupers of us all, the election to come will be fought on the trans issue and how many Meghan Markles can dance on the head of a pin.

Of course, Boomers aren't the problem, it is their cynical exploitation by financial interests.[1] The question is, should our democracy be so vulnerable to this phenomenon? With Liz Truss promising a 'bonfire of workers' rights', it's something to think about on the morning commute.

---

[1] I should have made this caveat earlier in the piece. The furious commentary from readers who had endured walking to school in the 1963 blizzard was chastening.

Not the Time

11 Sept 2022

There's a great deal you can't do today. You can't go to the football, the boxing, or the racing. You *can* go to the rugby in England, but not here in Wales. Cricket is acceptable everywhere. In jarring contrast to the start of the last Carolean era, a diktat from Marston's has outlawed music and dancing in Brains pubs for the next week. Christmas is, at time of publication, still scheduled to go ahead, fuel supplies permitting.

You may, if you wish, while away your weekend on social media, but I don't recommend it. Anything you post is prone to be condemned by a temporarily insane friend or relative.

'Here's a picture of the lovely sweet potato curry my wife made this evening.'

'Disgusting that you can think of eating at this difficult time. Shame on you.' – **RoyalBlue1956**

'Sweet potatoes have no place in a curry. Hugely emblematic of the casual racism that infects this imperialist hellhole. Shame on you.' – **SilentDisco2003**

Etc. etc. etc.

Those who are keen to observe correct etiquette will be glued to the BBC, watching the labyrinthine workings of constitutional upheaval.

'At 12.15 p.m. precisely, the Master of the Royal Guineafowl will unfurl the imperial bedspread in a tradition that traces back to Ethelred the Unhinged in 1013. Here's Giles Brandreth to explain what to expect.'

My personal all-time favourite royal moment was when our

new king allowed the microphones at Klosters to pick him up dissing Nicholas Witchell. At a time when the nation seems to be divided on every conceivable issue surely all of us, the rich man in his castle, the poor man at his gate, can coalesce around a healthy contempt for 'royal experts'. These shameless grifters are knocking out copy for the *Mail* and *Express* at such a rate that a cynic might suspect they had much of it written in advance. Your Majesty, you now have a tower with Beefeaters and ravens at your disposal, do us all a favour and put it to use.

You see, then, that the mad and the bad in the UK are not at a loss as to what to do this weekend. From those engaged in performative mourning/disrespect to others who are exploiting the situation professionally, the outliers of society are having a busy time. The vast majority of us, I'll suggest, feel some degree of sadness on a personal level and a deal of discomfort at the confusion about what is appropriate behaviour.

Take Adam Price, for example. For a little while on Thursday and Friday there was no Prince of Wales. There's no constitutional requirement for there to be one and Charles III didn't receive the title until long after his mother's accession. The Duke of Cambridge, however, has already been installed.

'There will be time, in due course, for a public debate surrounding the title of the Prince of Wales.' Price tweeted in response to the decision. But there won't, will there, butt? While you were stood at the buffet wondering if it was impolite to have a vol-au-vent, the hog roast has been chopped up and devoured.

And this is the genius of the British state. At the very point when change seems appropriate, or even necessary, the machine appears in human form and demands common decency from us. Even as the wheels continue to turn, it appeals to our humanity and begs for silence.

There are babies a week old who have lived through two premierships and two reigns. These are extremely precarious times for the UK and its nations. Saying and doing nothing might seem a safe option, but we do so at the risk of being spoken for against our interests.

Borderlands

27 February 2022

I had planned to report on this game from England. The idea was to find the leafiest, most cut-glass sounding venue I could – Beaumont-Super-Care RFC perhaps, demand a pint of Brains Skull Attack and engage the members on recent results against Scotland. Then Wayne Pivac dropped Rees-Zammit. I understand the rationale for this, he's not been on his best form, and we needed a physical presence in defence. But damn it, Zammit? A confident Wales would always field a winger like him, in the belief that whatever he let in would be repaid doubly by his attacking threat. So, I pulled up short of the border and took up a perch at the Old Nag's Head in Monmouth.

Border towns, the world over, have a unique vibe, don't they? Whether you're in Tijuana, Amritsar or Oswestry you'll find mangled accents, complex loyalties and enigmatic transients. Before the game, nobody had a clear vision of the outcome. Lloyd has concerns about the Welsh setup.

'It's going to be a tough couple of years for them. The Taine Basham generation will come through, but until they get some caps under their belts it's going to be hard. They've got no out and out 12/13 combination and that's crucial in the modern game.'

Matt, meanwhile, was more optimistic. Here was a classic border town character: marooned in his native Wales by Covid restrictions, he owns a bar called the Welsh Dragon in Wellington, New Zealand and seemed to have absorbed his adopted nation's quiet perspicacity about the sport.

'Neither side is on their A game; they are both misfiring. I see Wales edging it in a low-scoring match.'

As English penalties started going over, cheering roared across the bar from the smaller front room where white jerseys dominated. We clapped politely after each and shouted 'Come on Wales' loudly to demonstrate support *and* moral rectitude in the face of adversity. Wales were doing unexpected things well, forcing a scrum penalty in the opening minutes, for instance. The last time that happened at Twickenham, Peter West twisted a vowel and had to be stretchered out of the BBC studio. This was on ITV, however, where the sainted Shane is permitted to congratulate 'our forwards'.

The breakdown was England's and infringements left them ahead by 12 unanswered points at half-time. So, when England were gifted a try three minutes into the second half, the outlook was bleak. Referee Mike Adamson, notably punctilious about the most minor Welsh infringements in the first half, somehow managed to miss Maro Itoje barging Adam Beard out of a defensive lineout, leaving the line at Alex Dombrandt's mercy.[1]

Rugby, however, Matt explained, is like life: you live it in four quarters. For the first 20 minutes you don't know what's happening, just like a child. The second quarter is where you find your feet and decide how to prosper, as we do in our 20s and 30s. After half-time, you score points by accumulating assets and this sets you up for the final quarter of the game. You hope to make 80 minutes, and if there's any extra, that's a bonus.

And after the disputed England try, Wales began to build on the best aspects of their play in the first half. At the centre of their efforts, Taulupe Faletau made a mockery of predictions that he'd fade as the game wore on and played with increasing authority. Dogged at the breakdown, he also became an attacking threat, skilfully negotiating contact so that yards were gained each time he was held up. Josh Adams scooped up a difficult delivery for

---

[1] Having a crack at proper sports reporting here and immediately slipping into cliché. I was considering buying a sheepskin jacket at the time.

Wales' first try and the manner in which he took it should end any debate over which position this consummate wing threequarter should play.

Even after Nick Tompkins sliced through the English defence to leave Wales five points behind, there was a feeling that too high a mountain had been left to climb. Joe Marler's appearance on the field coincided with a more committed effort from England, and despite hope lingering into overtime, the physicality and discipline England displayed earned them a four-point victory.

Statistically, Alex Cuthbert was Wales' most effective attacker, notching up 17 metres in the game and justifying his inclusion at the expense of Rees-Zammit. If Wales really are in the borderlands between the Alun Wyn Jones and Taine Basham eras, it's concerning that Faletau and Cuthbert were the standouts here. They won't be reliable forever.

In Monmouth, most were happy with the performance.

'Why can't we start better?' asked Tony, who had sat quietly and rapt throughout the game. Well, that has to be down to confidence, and the selection policy doesn't seem to be geared towards fostering that. We have lost two from three and have no idea who will be playing in the centres or back row when France visit. I appreciate a transient atmosphere but, travelling back to Cardiff, couldn't help but wish for more clarity of purpose from a coaching team whose reputation is, I suspect, being saved by the native wit of their players.

All the World's a Stage

18 Sept 2022

I wonder if, after Statey Funes on Monday, we might be permitted to prevail upon the UK government to do a spot of governing for a while? After Brexit, lockdown, Platty Jubes, The Continuing Story of Bungalow Boris, Tory *X Factor*, and the Russia-Ukraine war, you'd think that a spell of mundane statecraft might appeal to our masters, if only for the novelty value.

When I was a boy, a minister would come home from work, take of his top hat and reassure the servants that he'd managed to keep us on the gold standard despite the unstable outlook for jute prices. Before leaving for a weekend's horseplay with the ghillies at his Highland estate, he might place a call to the Archbishop of Canterbury and register his concern at the moral decline of the nation, as evidenced by the unkempt appearance of a railway guard he'd had cause to rebuke on his journey home.

From that historically accurate reminiscence, only the top hat persists owing to the baffling presence in national life of Jacob Rees-Mogg: a man whose removal from the scene could be justified in terms of feng shui, bereft as he is of both utility and the potential to spark joy. But he looks memorable and can generate a meaningless controversy on demand, and these are the stocks in trade of the modern governing class.

I've always been rather scathing about Labour supporters pointing at Sure Start centres as a concrete achievement of the Blair government. In this scenario, Blair is Fred West, Sure Start centres are his patio and underneath it lies the Iraq War. They did, however fleetingly, actually exist in real life and I can't think of a tangible government-led project since.

When Johnson made his resignation speech, back in Elizabethan times, he listed his achievements thus:

- Won the biggest majority since 1987.
- Delivered Brexit.
- Delivered manifesto commitments including social care.
- Helped people up and down the country.
- Ensured Britain stands tall in the world.
- Spoken with clarity and authority.

Now, I'm sure you've all undergone a job interview or annual appraisal at one time or another. How far do you reckon you'd have got with this sort of vague, evidence-free spiel? Leaving aside the blatant lie about social care, the only specific achievement listed is delivering Brexit. The problem here is that Brexit isn't a thing, it's the absence of a thing: membership of the European Union. The only specific item of delivery listed is a void.

All this would make some sense if a series of projects had failed over the last couple of decades. The 2008 crash or the pandemic could safely be blamed for derailing governmental ambitions. In reality, though, policy has ceased to represent any genuine intentions and, instead, is frequently invented on the hoof as a distraction from whatever chaos is consuming the nation in a given week. During the Tory leadership campaign both candidates stated enthusiasm for the Rwanda deportation policy and pledged to extend it further. You know the policy is a fiction, they know it, Rwanda knows it and the asylum seekers who continue to arrive in Kent know it. It exists purely as theatre for the handful of voters in swing seats who can keep the actors on the stage.

Harold Macmillan warned prospective leaders about the disruptive potential of 'events, dear boy', but without events our current politicians would have nothing at all to justify their existence. Johnson's enthusiasm for the war in Ukraine epitomised the way that crises have become the meat and potatoes of politicians who have no aptitude nor inclination to get on with running the country. Politicians *look* busy during cataclysmic events, but the decisions largely make themselves and any errors can be blamed on officials.

Conveniently, neglect of the nation's management ensures that crises occur on an ever more regular basis, so it is 'not the time' to discuss anything that requires planning and hard work virtually all of the time. Gaps between crises can be covered in the news cycle by fantasy announcements like the Rwanda flights or a bridge between Scotland and Ireland.

Many have spoken this week of how the ceremonial spectacle in London has made them proud to be British. The spectacle may be all there is left.[1]

---

[1] Guy Debord is alive and unwell in Rhondda Fach.

The Banality of Evil

29 Jan 2023

Each Monday I resolve that this week's column won't be yet another attack on the Tories. As a youth, I witnessed Ben Elton's Friday Night Live routines decay until he was content merely to abbreviate the Prime Minister's name for the entertainment of those she had culturally diminished.

'Mrs Thatcher, eh?'

'What about Mrs Thatch?'

'Thatch!!'

I don't want to be like that. I want to be proper erudite and bring a critical eye to all facets of society. Elton, of course, went on to pen a musical with Tory peer and purveyor of top-class entertainment, Andrew Lloyd-Webber, noting that,

'If I were to refuse to talk to Tories, I would narrow my social and professional scope considerably. If you judge all your relationships on a person's voting intentions, I think you miss out on the varieties of life.'

I should acknowledge that Elton had rather more at stake than I do. My 'social scope' consists of Mrs W, the bloke in Happy Shopper who sells me my fags, and a monthly phone call from Greasy Tony – a car enthusiast with whom I used to sell double glazing in 1994. So, all-in-all, I've got no business being sniffy about befriending Tories, I might learn something.

The trouble is you just don't get Andrew Lloyd Webber grade Tories anymore. He resigned from the Lords in 2017 to devote more time developing Avant Garde facial expressions. If I were to collaborate on a West End spectacular with a Tory tunesmith, I'd have to choose between Phil Collins and Gary Numan. My libretto for *Andrew RT Davies: The Opera* seems destined to never to be put to music.

Arty types, you see, tend to possess a sliver of common feeling for wider humanity, even if their usual experience of it is in servitude. You can't parlay your ripped-off Verdi melodies into successful theatrical juggernauts without having a vague idea of how the bovine masses respond to emotional stimuli. Neither can you squeeze your septuagenarian fundament into leopard skin trousers and shake it convincingly for stadiums full of HRT-fuelled rock chicks if the only public reaction you've ever experienced is revulsion.

Torydom has jumped the shark from politically obnoxious to culturally unacceptable. It has gone from being the ice bucket challenge in 2019 to driving under the influence of ketamine in 2023.

During a debate this week on migrant children who have gone missing, Tory MP Jonathan Gullis shouted,

'They shouldn't have come here illegally, then!'

Who, apart from the absolute dregs of society, can identify with that sentiment? The Tory Party used to hold such wide appeal because it appealed to the individualist within all of us. Even the worthiest yoghurt-knitting Lefty harbours selfish impulses and the Selfservatives existed to nurture those and provide a sheen of respectability for acting on them. Becoming a buy-to-let landlord? Nothing wrong with that, you are providing housing for the nation, well done!

Gullis and his ilk don't represent any normal facet of human experience. A psychologist might look at his utterances and suspect a deep well of self-hatred and that simply isn't part of the makeup of most people.

During the Brexit campaign, I grew rather weary of people saying we were flirting with fascism. It seemed alarmist and gauche, redolent of Rik from *The Young Ones* – a Ben Elton creation. But what can I say to those people now? I'm forced on to the topic of Tory depravity week on week because they continue to plunge further into it with seemingly nobody in their midst left to object.

Make It New!

2 Oct 2022

Writing behind the *Telegraph*'s paywall, avant-garde economist, Kwasi Kwarteng, has conceded that not all the measures he announced last week would be 'universally popular'. 'We had no choice,' explained the cabinet's Marcel Duchamp, swiftly secreting an OBR forecast in the *pissoir* he has refashioned as a briefcase. 'We had to do something different.'

'At least you guys get me,' the Chancellor continued. 'Without the underground press, I worry there just wouldn't be a cultural space for fiscal expressionism that rejects the tired old tropes of home ownership and nutrition-to-respiration ratios.'

Citing Yoko Ono and Sun Ra as his primary influences, Kwarteng has been chafing against convention since his Eton days where, famously, he turned up to the Founder's Day eel feast having modified his top hat with a 'F*** the Pound!' badge.

'Those were crazy days,' Kwarteng snorts. 'You have to remember that guys like Darius Guppy and Bear Grylls were legends at the school's Economics Society. So, right there, I had a sense of what was possible, from subverting the norms of the insurance market to surviving on your own urine. I knew instinctively that I had to go further.'

Kwarteng defends the right of the artist to reinvent himself at will.

'I might wake up one day and think, you know, just because nobody has ever funded tax cuts with borrowed money before doesn't mean I can't give it a whirl and see where the chips fall.' Pausing to replay Lou Reed's *Metal Machine Music*, which he favours in the background when thinking, the Chancellor stares distantly out of his Treasury office window.

'You know, there comes a time when bold decisions have to be made. When you think of the failed statesmen of the past, such as Nero, they listened to bad advice. Without that horse of budgetary responsibility, we might all be speaking Latin!'

Asked if this iconoclasm is at odds with the critique of British colonial rule he provided in his book, *Ghosts of Empire*, Kwarteng's mood darkens. Snatching a copy from the shelf, he reads aloud,

'The reliance on individual administrators to conceive and execute policy with very little strategic direction from London often led to contradictory and self-defeating policies, which in turn brought disaster to millions.'

Replacing the book on the shelf next to Ezra Pound's *Make it New*, he screams,

'2011 I wrote that! You might as well expect Ant & Dec still to be appearing in *Byker Grove*.'

Replacing Lou Reed with The Shamen's 'Ebeneezer Goode', the chancellor warms to his theme.

'Only in annihilation is renewal possible. From death comes life in the relentless cycle of chaotic revolution to which we must all submit. As an artist and economist, I am bound by a sacred oath to tear the fabric of what has gone before and start anew. I am Shiva: Destroyer of Worlds.'

'Don't forget about pork markets,' comes a voice from next door.

Meanwhile, at the Labour conference, Sir Keir Starmer unveiled a freshly commissioned photograph of a 2013 Toyota Yaris which, he insists, will be attainable to all under Labour, provided we behave ourselves.

A Statement from the Anti-Growth Coalition

9 Oct 2022

Here at the Anti-Growth Coalition, we have mixed feelings about our work suddenly coming under the public spotlight. Prior to this week's speech by the prime minister, we had been used to going about our business quietly and without fuss. As luck would have it, the speech coincided with the AGC's AGM and the joke amongst delegates was that we were so obscure, there was a danger the public might think that the PM had invented us. LOL!

But no, we are very real and, much as it goes against our instincts, now is the time to reveal our workings to the world at large. Some might assume that the crux of our philosophy is a deep, burning resentment at those who have worked hard and prospered in life. The truth is more nuanced than that. Take transport for example. We have no quarrel with anybody driving a bus, train, ambulance, or fire engine for monetary gain. It is our belief that these people should qualify for a salary that permits them, not only to heat their homes, but to take their state-subsidised children for a mini-break to Center Parcs on a biannual basis.

Our problem is with the driving of white vans and private jets. Many have assumed that this antipathy is rooted in environmental concerns, but the truth is that these are far outweighed by the cultural disgust we feel towards those eternal bedfellows: bricklayers and hedge fund managers. Is there anything more vomit-inducing than settling in for a soy latte in the Islington Java Cooperative and having to listen to a gauche City type boasting about the tax contribution he's made this year? Well, yes actually, it's being subjected to a brickie's 'legitimate concerns about immigration' as he repoints the south-facing wall of your yoga studio.

The centrepiece of this year's conference was a round table discussion on growth suppression involving leading lights of our organisation from all walks of life. Ours is a broad coalition and we were delighted to welcome representatives from the Trades Union Congress, Metropolitan Police, all of the Judiciary, Stonewall, the National Trust, Greenpeace, the BBC (obvs), 85% of the populations of Wales and Scotland, the EU, the ECHR, the UN, Amnesty International, Sinn Fein, the House of Lords, the Church of England, and our sponsors, Ben & Jerry's.

All of us were united around our central theme: hatred of freedom and contempt for the late queen. Keynote speaker, the Duchess of Sussex, rallied the faithful with a passionate demand that Mick Lynch of the RMT be installed as monarch with absolute power to dispense justice to buy-to-let landlords and people who claim to know what a woman is.

Before a vote could even be taken, Chairman Gary Lineker brought down his gavel and declared the Duchess' motion passed, to chants of 'We hate democracy' from the Remoaner Alliance, headed on this occasion by Sir Nicholas Soames.[1]

Delegates were delighted by the intervention of Mark Drakeford who, having closed all the roads in the vicinity, invited the assembled to board helicopters from President Emeritus, Greta Thunberg's private fleet and fly them through the Brynglas tunnels at rush hour. Detouring to the Prince of Wales Bridge, Drakeford landed his craft and constructed a makeshift checkpoint from unused Covid testing kits before spray painting *Cymru am byth!* across the bridge's signage and high-fiving Gerry Adams.

---

[1]Government scapegoating, had by this point, extended to nearly every public figure in the UK. The only blameless actors were the government itself and people who intended to vote for them. Everyone else was the enemy within.

If Liz Truss wants a scrap then, believe me, we at the Anti-Growth Coalition are ready and able for the fight. From Vladimir Putin to Lily Allen, we are committed to tearing apart all she holds dear and ushering into reality a new Britain in which 12 years of uninterrupted Tory rule is no barrier to imagining everything must be somebody else's fault.

Players Gonna Play

16 Oct 2022

If you've ever played chess, you'll be familiar with the feeling that accompanies the realisation that you are definitely going to lose. Scouring the board for non-existent escape routes, the best you can do is delay the inevitable by pointlessly sacrificing a bishop and moving a pawn forward. If only you hadn't lost your queen so early in the game. As your humiliation unfolds, you rather wish you'd opted to play something more suited to your abilities, KerPlunk! perhaps.

It's fair to say, I think, that amongst Vladimir Putin's more vocal critics, he probably has more respect for the strategic abilities of Garry Kasparov than those of Grandmaster Truss. For whilst Gazza the Brain famously lost humanity's mastery of chess to a computer, he was, at least, aware of his opponent. Liz Truss appears to be playing against herself and losing from both sides.

Amidst the hot takes and viral memes that have cheered the nation during the events of this week, we seem to be wilfully distracted from the terrifying context in which our ruling class is disgracing itself. Imagine being a democracy campaigner in China and watching the Westminster pantomime. Your government tells its people that liberal democracy can only guarantee chaos and the seizure of power by an economic elite. The UK's slide into ungovernable rancour and poverty serves as the perfect example of what they mean. If you visit the Public Gallery at the House of Commons, you are handed a leaflet explaining that the process you are witnessing is the gold standard of government by the people. Now, with that concept under genuine global threat, our system has degraded to a point of such grotesque deformity that no nation on earth would consider adopting it.

In a capitalist society, the prime functions of government are to provide investors with the conditions in which they can make a profit, whilst protecting the population from exploitation. We are now so far beyond the looking glass that the markets have to protect us from the government as it is in danger of leaving us unfit for exploitation. Whitehall gossip has it that Truss fired Kwarteng because he wanted to fully reverse the planned cut in Capital Gains Tax whilst she favoured a partial adjustment to the policy. Once it became clear that Sterling would plummet unless she did as he advised, he was fired anyway on the basis that someone had to carry the can. When Truss announced the reversal, the pound fell again *during the press conference* purely as a reaction to her nakedly incompetent presentation. This, remember, is a prime minister with no national mandate whatsoever, and who refuses to engage with the elected heads of the devolved governments. If you think you can hear something sinister in the night, that will be the distant echo of Xi Jinping laughing.

So, what now? Jeremy Hunt is the *de facto* prime minister and will announce a budget on Halloween (more hilarious memes) in which he'll attempt to plug the remaining £40 billion hole in public finances with tax rises and cuts to public services. As with Kwarteng's fiscal event of the season, none of these measures will ever have been before the electorate and will bear no relation to the manifesto upon which Boris Johnson won an election and subsequently ignored. Regrettably, the 2019 Red Wall Tory voters will find they are not being levelled up after all. If you would like to contribute to the 'Send a Class Traitor a Tiny Violin' fundraiser this Christmas, then have a word with yourself.

We have seen the parameters within which our democracy is allowed to work this week. The markets have reversed government policy with a few keystrokes. That nobody is outraged about this shows how far from accountability the system allows our leaders to stray. Without a mandate, they are no more our representatives than the gilt traders who halted their folly on Friday. A general election may change the colour of the pieces, but unless the game is played by people who respect the rules it will be checkmate for liberal democracy.

The Age of Aquarius

23 Oct 2022

You'd imagine that whatever passes for Liz Truss's friends are rallying around her this weekend, proffering Prosecco and Gloria Gaynor CDs.

'The worst is over, babes. The UK never deserved you...'

Nobody could deny the second part of that, but as the press fixates on the possibility of us getting back together with our toxic ex, it could be that Liz's nightmare has only just begun.

As the Age of Pisces draws to a close, we can expect to see the rehabilitation of horned beasts in the iconography of the world. After 2000 years of representing evil, the mantle will pass to fish as we transfer our revulsion for anything to do with Aries the ram to Piscean imagery and rush headlong into the Age of Aquarius.

The passing of an Age demands the active rejection of its predecessor, which is why the devil has horns and Christians have stickers of fish on their cars.

Alright Russell Grant, you might ask, but what has this got to do with Liz Truss?

Liz stands at the intersecting point of two paths of history: the demographic shift that will see Millennials outnumbering Baby Boomers at the ballot box, and the global unravelling of trickledown economics as a credible theory.

She wasn't undone by personal scandal like Boris and didn't even have time to generate the sort of negative polling figures that saw the words 'Ian Duncan-Smith' assume the marketing appeal of botulism. Her sensational bum's rush was rooted in ideology.

The UK has, for 40 years, broadly adhered to the cobbled together version of free market economics that Keith Joseph taught Margaret Thatcher in the mid-1970s. It has permeated national life so fully that its tenets have come to be accepted by most of the populace as facts of life and to challenge them has been to attract charges of blasphemy and trial by humiliation.

Whilst governments have varied in how devoutly they applied these ideas, any deviation has been explained as a regrettable emergency measure on the way to ideological purity.

It is telling that recent events have taken place during a long-running rail strike and against the backdrop of punishing energy prices.

Every schoolchild knows that the driving force of our economic system is competition. If you work hard at your lessons, you'll be able to secure a good job that allows you to save enough money to start your own business. Freed from the burden of high taxes, you, a striver, can then invest your profits in a new railway line that exactly follows the course of an existing line and upon which you can run more efficient trains. Over time, customers of the original train line will defect to your railway, and it will close down. This closure is a wonderful thing for society as it will allow you to take on all of its workers on zero hours contracts and thus leverage lower wages for your existing employees. Hey Presto! Your railway has become even *more* efficient.

Not every schoolchild dreams of running their own railway, though. Your buccaneering, entrepreneurial spirit might inspire you to start your own energy company. Don't be put off by the seemingly unsurmountable infrastructure challenges involved in developing a source of energy and delivering it to homes across the country. All that's been done for you with public money. Your role here is to devise a system of billing so opaque that your customers would require a PhD in statistics to work out whether or not they are being ripped off. Be sure to include a pastel abstract of a tree at the top of their bills, along with a strapline saying something like 'Good Nature – Delivering Green Gas to Children.'

Truss arrived at the very point when the cruel absurdity of Tory economics had finally allowed space for people like the RMT's Mick Lynch to receive a fair hearing from the public. In attempting to double down on its most ludicrous premise: prosperity for all can only be achieved if the rich get richer, she became the embodiment of an idea whose time had passed. From here on in, anybody suggesting the application of these policies will be met with a two-word response: 'Liz Truss.'

So, dry your eyes babes, you'll need them to comprehend the true horror of your situation.

Liz Truss is the new Arthur Scargill.

A Life Less Ordinary

12 March 2022

If you claim to know what's going on with the Wales team, you are one of three things:

- A liar
- *Twp*
- Wayne Pivac

Until this week, the only reliable element to the Six Nations story was that Wales had discovered their next era-defining player in Taine Basham. We're in *transition* we all nodded over our consolatory pints, after all it's not a World Cup year and these young players are gaining invaluable experience…

But Basham, like Rees-Zammit a couple of weeks ago, apparently needed bringing down a peg or two. Or three, as he was dismissed from the match-day squad altogether and sent home to contemplate the folly of allowing himself to be touted as a future British Lion.

Alun Wyn Jones, we learned, had returned to the squad to train. He wasn't *in* the squad, but an aura of Alun-ness had returned to the setup as they prepared to face the most highly rated French side we've seen in years.

I visited Llanidloes RFC for this game. Nestled in the Cambrian hills, and untroubled by a railway line since 1962, Llani attracts people who like to be left to their own devices and dream up a life less ordinary. Wayne Pivac would love it here. Nobody held out much hope. The imperious French pack seemed bound to take us apart at the breakdown and starve our backs of possession. Had the game been played on a standard, drizzly Saturday afternoon that logic might well have held firm, But Friday night in the 'diff always has the potential to astound if you do it properly and, from the off, Wales were up for a scrap.

A bracingly physical encounter drew gasps from the assembled. After Atonio emerged with the ball from one collision, Peadar, whose Irishness is painted red for four games out of five, looked awestruck.

'He's like a *pissoir* with a beard!'

The French try nine minutes in seemed ominous. All the 'death of Welsh rugby' warnings we'd heard after the Ireland game seemed once again apposite as we stared a drubbing in the face. But this is Dan Biggar's team, and he does not do capitulation. Vocal as ever, he roared his pack on to dominance, rewarding them with long strolls forward as he rifled in perfect kicks to control territory.

At half-time, it seemed to me that we'd got the measure of this. The sheer intensity of Wales' work at the breakdown meant that France were playing to our tune, tries would surely come. France, however, had a telling advantage. I've watched this series in Cardiff, Cardigan, Monmouth and Powys, and one name has been invoked everywhere I've been. It's somewhat extraordinary that a defence coach from Wigan should dominate talk of Welsh rugby years after he left the WRU's employ. Such is the impact that Shaun Edwards had on our national game, and as Wales hurled everything at the French line last night, I'll wager that his was the most mentioned name in the country. Wales *were* the better side, but France don't need to be good to win, when push comes to shove, they can defend a lead for as long as it takes.

So, where are we now? Rees-Zammit was allowed off the naughty step to try and unpick Edwards' system towards the end, but if he was the solution why knock his confidence by dropping him? Faletau remains superb but nobody knows our back row from one game to the next. At the outset of the tournament, it seemed that we were building for the future, with Basham assuming a central role and Dan Biggar given licence to inspire the team in his own image. Now, AWJ is touted to play against Italy and, with nothing left to play for, we seem to be looking back to past glories. If Wales play as well as they did last night, they will post a cricket score next week but I'm at a loss to know what has been achieved in terms of moulding these fine players into a coherent entity. We hope that Wayne Pivac has a plan, because tenacity and spirit won't allay catastrophe forever.

A Master Songwriter of the Hills

14 Aug 2023

Songwriter Andrew Hawkey's living room in Llanidloes is a temple of erudition. Books line one wall, whilst another holds the meticulously curated vinyl collection that charts his progress through life. There are records of glorious obscurity here: songwriters who once burned with something to say to a world that barely listened. Some, like Townes Van Zandt (signed, original pressing), found a mass audience posthumously whilst others, like Bob Carpenter, sunk without trace entirely, save for the preservation of their work in this room.

Slight, intense, and immaculate, Andrew wears his years with apparent insouciance. There's eight decades of experience and stories on offer, if you ask, but this is a man with his eyes on the future, still restlessly exploring a creative urge that demands as much of him as it ever did. 2015 saw him issue *What Did I Come Up Here For?* – a reflective collection of songs that, at the time, he felt might be his last. However, radio play and critical acclaim for the craftsmanship of songs like 'Apple Green' stiffened his sinews and *Long Story Short*, a muscular set that is every bit the equal of its influences, crept out during the pandemic.

It can often feel that Americana is a rather contrived genre. Born at the turn of this century to market alt-country acts in which Nashville had no interest, it has grown to accommodate any artist who draws on the roots of American popular music to flavour their songwriting. On both sides of the Atlantic the niche has endless space for earnest plaid-shirted thirtysomethings as they dignify the end of their indie youth by setting off in search of 'authenticity'. It is a quasi-religious quest and the tropes of its deities – Townes, The Band, Emmylou Harris, John Fahey, Gene

Clark etc. – echo around that corner of contemporary music like a catechism.

Andrew wouldn't be seen dead in a plaid shirt and his authenticity as a storyteller is underpinned by a life lived in defiance of convention. A boarding school education designed to usher him into middle-class respectability instead left him restless and mistrustful of authority. There is a searching quality to his songs that betrays a vocation to explore the margins of experience.

After some besuited years selling houses in the early 1970s London property boom, including a spell for Roy Brooks, a self-described Communist famous for his honest adverts[1], Andrew joined the countercultural emigration to rural Wales. Landing first in Pontarfynach, he spent the years until 1985 in a series of remote, unconverted farm cottages, at one point having to flee a blizzard and walk to the coast. Reflecting on life with no electricity, telephone or plumbing he smiles, 'I can still smell the Elsan from the chemical toilets.'

Listening to tracks from that period on his recent compilation *Hindsight: Andrew Hawkey at 80*, I'm struck by uncompromising commitment to songcraft. Some songs had the potential to be stretched from folk into prog territory at a time when the market liked that sort of thing. Others could have been polished into pop material, leaning on the strong melodies that characterise this work. Instead, the compilation presents a set of taut songs that are arranged simply and don't beg for attention. In other words, they offer the stripped-back aesthetics of contemporary Americana and consequently sound fresh today.

The set kicks off with the yearning 'Between Two Horizons' which showcases Andrew as a sweet-voiced youth full of concern

---

[1] E.g. '£5995! Broken-down Battersea bargain. Erected at the end of a long reign of increasingly warped moral and aesthetic values, it's what you expect – hideous...'

and uncertainty. Recorded in 1969, before his move to Elenydd, it's poignant to hear him singing to us from the dog days of the 1960s, wondering what's next. Arranged chronologically, the album answers that question, and we hear the voice filling out, the themes deepening, and the emergence of a goatish charm that characterises his live performances to this day.

The final two tracks round the collection out into a satisfying narrative. 'Spirit', from 2020's *Long Story Short* has Andrew, then 78, being inspired by young idealists around him in Llanidloes. Spiralling through the years, he interrogates whether he's lived up to his beliefs.

'Looking back is similar to the non-sequitur nature of dreaming,' he tells me in a voice that translates to his singing: precise and melodious with a hint of Cornish fruit. 'Nothing is what we planned on the thin ice of life.'

These songs have a tendency to undercut themselves. They are never content to reduce life to simplicity, whatever is there needs to be weighed, peered at and poked so that its complexity can be revealed. Andrew habitually uses EADGAD tuning on his 12-string guitar. This produces chord voicings that seem to question along with the lyrics. It also means that chords often don't resolve, hanging wistfully in the mix as a reminder that there's always more to learn.

The final track is a return to the opener, 'Between Two Horizons'. Re-recorded for the album, it gives us a man trying out his old convictions to see if they still convince. They convince me, and key to this is that Andrew has lived by them. The hippies, for want of a better word, who settled in rural Wales *and stayed* had to find a way to make their ideals compatible with the culture they moved to. Any faddish notions of life in the hills melt away when winter sets in and you need assistance from sheep farmers whose respect is reserved for hard work and correct behaviour in the pub. Most returned to England with a tale to tell, including dozens of musicians who promised to create a new society in 'the country' only to be found out as tourists. Those who dug in to make it work had their beliefs stress tested. Andrew is one of those and it's evident in his music, which could never have been made for London nightclubs. It's the work of a man who knows how to handle solitude.

He remains a quester; currently he's excited to discover the benefits of Cranial Sacral Therapy, but has also put his roadwork in. For 20 years he criss-crossed Wales and beyond, playing over 1000 shows on keyboards for Pat Grover's Blues Zeros, 'Five middle-class white men with an embarrassing hellhound problem,' as Andrew has it. *Hindsight* includes a live recording of Sonny Boy Williamson's 'Help Me' from 1994 in the demanding setting of Newbridge Memo Club. It's fine, sweaty blues that's a world away from Andrew's more delicate compositions, but equally representative of his personality. On *Long Story Short* he has, in 'Jones On Me', a smoky slice of sly, sexual cheekiness that he'll tell you is ironic. Well, maybe.

If you were to put Andrew on a Spotify playlist it would probably fall under 'Americana'. This music, though, is more like source material from which exponents of that genre could draw. It is a seam of creativity, stretching from the counterculture to now, that should be reckoned with by anyone who loves songs for their own sake.

Asked for a summation of his musical life, Andrew considers the matter for a good while before offering,

'When I failed, I still fought to the last barricade.'

Satisfied for a moment, he smiles before narrowing his eyes.

'Did I really, though?'[2]

---

[2] Andrew Hawkey's albums can be ordered from www.andrew-hawkey-music.co.uk

What's He Doing There?

30 Oct 2022

You can relax now; we have awoken from the Trussian nightmare, and everything is back to normal. The UK citizenry was understandably incensed by crazed idealogues seizing the levers of government and crashing the economy, so it is comforting to know that we are once again safe in the hands of cold-eyed, market-approved operatives who can be trusted to euthanise our dreams gradually and with a veneer of compassion.

Is life going to be worse? Of course it is! How could things get better if they didn't get worse in the first place? If things didn't get worse, we wouldn't need politicians at all, and then where would we be? Worse is the crucial ingredient of hope, and hope can only be created by skilled politicians who can manufacture it from despair.

'Everything is awful!' the politician explains. 'You and your children are on the brink of starvation!'

They have our attention. We draw our children closer…

'But behold, I am here, and all will be well!'

Our children look up at us expectantly…

'But first, things must get worse…'

The election of Liz Truss was only possible because the electorate was small enough, and insane enough, to be impervious to outside influence of any sort. With her defenestration, it must be salutary for Tory members to realise that even their entitlement is no longer sufficient to see their votes count in 21st-Century Britain. Like the rest of us, they must be looking at Rishi Sunak and

Jeremy Hunt and wondering how the hell they got there.

The fear must be that we are allowing unprecedented erosion of our civic culture because we are too collectively traumatised to do anything about it. The last election was less than three years ago, but that strange Christmas when Boris Johnson did his creepy John Lewis advert is separated from us by a pandemic that killed hundreds of thousands and a series of emergency measures that required us to surrender every vestige of personal freedom.

I still sometimes reflexively reach for a non-existent mask when entering a building. That sort of practice becomes embedded, as does the acceptance that leadership being imposed upon us is justified by crisis. If this were the case then democracy could be suspended indefinitely as long as crises were continually manufactured... oh, hang on...

So, as our government has been appointed by market extortion, we should at least be curious enough to try to make sense of what it actually wants to do. The answer to this seems to be depressingly simple: give our money to the markets. Whodathunkit?

The only substantive change on offer from the new regime is a promise of 'fiscal responsibility' – for which read austerity. Other batshit elements of the Truss dystopia have been retained as a sop to the newly disenfranchised membership. The cap on bankers' bonuses will still be lifted (colour me shocked), Brexit remains an article of faith which must not be questioned, and immigration still features as the national scapegoat.

Anyone hoping that the environment would receive more serious attention from the new PM will have adjusted their expectations upon hearing that he's not going to bother showing up to next week's COP27. Neither is he allowing an appearance by regal yoghurt knitter, King Charles. To underscore his 'burn baby burn' attitude to the issue, Sunak has appointed cigar-chomping shambles Therese Coffey to head up DEFRA.

Mark Drakeford, we are assured, has received a telephone call from the Prime Minister. Reports that the mandate-rich First Minister threatened to 'do you like I done Davies in the Senedd' remain unconfirmed at press time.[1]

But there has to be a narrative of change. While the reality of this government is that it will drip-bleed our wages to satisfy market demands, the press has been content to go with the diversity angle. A glance at Twitter will reveal *Spectator* hacks and GB News propagandists hailing the dawn of multicultural Britain with the blood of Sadiq Khan still drying around their mouths. Suella Braverman, they tell us, is a Buddhist, presumably the sort of Buddhist who compassionately sweeps ants from her path and on to privately chartered jets to Rwanda.

But who do we blame now? When Johnson was treating the country as a playpen for his extended toddlerhood, we could point at the Brexit-addled voters in England who fell for his sweaty advances. It was the reliably incorrect Tory membership that foisted Liz Truss upon us. This time, the author of our misery has been voted for by precisely nobody. Even Tory MPs ended up with no choice. If we quietly acquiesce to this, we have nobody to blame but ourselves.[2]

---

[1] Mild-mannered Mark Drakeford had recently become so incensed at Andrew RT Davies during First Minister's questions, that he had begun shaking with rage and throwing paperwork around. For a glorious moment it looked like he might secure his place in history by decking him.
[2] Spoiler alert: we did.

Leaky Sue

6 Nov 2022

I'm going to break this down very simply. When a country is invaded, it is justified to use force against the invading forces. Home Secretary Suella Braverman chose to characterise the arrival of migrants on the south coast of England as an 'invasion' *three days* after Andrew Leak, 66, threw firebombs at an immigration processing centre in Dover. What possible interpretation can there be for her language, other than that the attack was, if not justified, then rationally explicable?

In the days between the attack and the Home Secretary's intervention, disgraced former UKIP leader Henry Bolton sought to explain the attack as an expression of 'frustration' at the Home Office's failure to deal with small craft landing in Kent.

There was a time when the Conservative Party's remit included a commitment to upholding robust patriotic values as a bulwark against dangerous nationalism. For all your racist uncle's 'Enoch was right' grumbling, Powell was never given sway over a party that recognised the fine line it needed to tread. He exiled himself into Ulster unionism: an early indicator of what a blind alley that would turn out to be.

Similarly, despite his profile, Nigel Farage has failed to find a place at the top table of British politics.

Now, however, we have a Home Secretary who looks at the repellent utterances of Bolton *et al* and seeks not only to legitimise them, but to exceed their potential to inflame.

Clearly delighting in her notoriety, Braverman chose to visit Kent in a Chinook helicopter later in the week.

Braverman's behaviour is explicable in two ways. Firstly, she is under intense pressure to resign again or be sacked over her cavalier stewardship of government documents. It makes sense for her to change the narrative by any means necessary, but also to throw red meat to the *Daily Mail* readership who can be relied upon to view her removal as a 'woke' betrayal of the insane values that their end of the country has adopted to distract from the obvious failure of Brexit.

Braverman, though, is no actress. Plenty of Tories have resorted to base populism when their backs have been against the wall, only to return to the status quo when the pressure was off. Leaky Sue, however, means every word. So, how has the Tory Party got into a position whereby its historical refusal to merge with the far right is so imperilled?

For the answer to that you need to stare into the haunted eyes of Jeremy Hunt. While Rishi Sunak can't hide his delight at being made Head Boy once again, Hunt has the look of a man charged with dire responsibilities. It is being widely briefed that next week the Chancellor will impose taxes on second homes and share dividends. He's also predicted to raise capital gains tax. This will place the government far to the left of Keir Starmer's Labour Party on the economy, completing a five-week journey for the Tories from Kwasi Kwarteng's Reaganomic wonderland to a strange new home next door to John McDonnell.

In the light of this people will rightly ask what the Conservative Party is *for*? The free market couldn't thrive during Covid, neither has it responded to Brexit as we were promised it would. Privatised entities from rail to the utilities are increasingly reliant on state intervention and we are all receiving seemingly random payments from the government in an attempt to keep the country afloat.

As the economic ethos of modern conservatism is abandoned in this chaos, its proponents have nowhere to turn but the scapegoating of migrants and the civil servants charged with administering failed policies.

The Manston migrant centre, which is meant for 1600 people and currently holds over 4000, has seen outbreaks of diphtheria and MRSA amongst its unfortunate residents. Violence has become endemic and despite a supposed maximum stay of 24 hours, some families have been sleeping on the floor for over a month.

The plight of refugees isn't a problem of the country's governance, it is an emblem of it. Failed economic theories and a kleptocratic ruling class have left the UK on the verge of financial ruin and the conditions in Manston are a microcosm of the wrecked public services that we are enduring up and down the country.

Sunak's willingness to accept Braverman as the price of support from MPs on the right of his party represents the final death of the Tory Party as we have known it. Her language is indistinguishable from the line taken by the British National Party in the early years of this century and reflective of the shrinking constituency to which Conservatives must appeal to remain viable.

A party that is content to trade on human misery as its sole appeal to voters is beyond hope and, from my perspective, beyond satire. The sheer ugliness of what is unfolding in our names at Westminster is a stain upon us all, and we must never forgive it.

Paradise Lost

20 March 2022

Some days Wales is a paradise and, waking up in glorious Powys sunshine, I set off down the A470 without the gnawing uncertainty that had accompanied the drizzle days of this year's Six Nations. It had been a confusing campaign, but Wales had shown their tenacity and the maths seemed to favour us today. A hatful of tries in Cardiff and we could finish third. Turning off towards Penderyn, I smiled at the wild horses on the Beacons and turned the stereo up. My perch for the game was the bar at the Cwm Farm Shop in Treorchy where I was joined by the Rhondda's renaissance man: writer, artist, singer, and retired prop, Siôn Tomos Owen.

Selection for the game, once again, baffled the nation. Much has been made about Wayne Pivac's willingness to make tough choices, as evidenced by the furloughing of Rees-Zammit and Taine Basham's summary dismissal. What to make, then, of this week's decision to demote our form forward, Will Rowlands, in favour of Alun Wyn Jones? Nobody begrudges AWJ running out for his 150th cap, but this felt like the sort of complacent sentimentality against which Pivac is supposed to stand.

Italy started brightly, but there didn't seem to be too much cause for concern.

'They always do,' Siôn noted. 'An initial thrust before they get knackered and the empire falls.'

There were familiar patterns to Wales' game, though, that were troubling. Once again, the Welsh pack was committing only one player to the ruck, and it wasn't proving fourth time lucky. Instead of providing a rapid platform for the backs, the tactic produced turnovers and penalties. Moreover, if your forwards aren't at the breakdown, you can't have them cluttering up the backline like photo-bombers in a wedding portrait. And the backs had their own woes. Standing so deep they were at forty-five degrees to the base of the scrum at times, it was taking three passes before they reached the gain line. This left much to the ingenuity of the wings and there were glimpses of Rees-Zammit's lofty abilities as he glided infield.

'He's like a greyhound,' Siôn explained, 'while Adams is a terrier and Cuthbert is a horse!'

And Wales do have a fabulous menagerie of attacking threequarters to choose from, which makes the seeming lack of organised moves all the more frustrating.

Owen Watkin jinked beautifully for a try to send Wales in at half-time and we were relaxed enough to grumble indulgently about the performance.

'What do reckon then, Siôn?'

'I'm...*baffled*! 12-7 behind to *Italy* in the last game of the season. Duw, Duw.'

It seemed okay though, not the joyous carnival of sunshine rugby we'd hoped for, but Welsh class would tell in the end, surely?

'We'll win on fitness while passing like Under-8s. Another pint, butt?'

The expected Italian capitulation wasn't happening, though. The opening 10 minutes of the second half were scruffy and when Dewi Lake flopped over the line for a try, reaction in Treorchy was muted as we watched the £100 ticket holders in the stadium spray understrength beer around like we'd won the World Cup. The Italian response was immediate, and it took a textbook winger's tackle from Josh Adams to prevent an end-to-end try from Italy's potent back three. A penalty saw them back into the lead anyway and we were reduced to diversionary conversation.

'I'm not a fan of the green socks,' Simon offered, 'they offend my sense of tradition.'

'The green socks are the only thing I like,' countered a morose Siôn.

With 10 minutes left, it was Adams again who brought the goods. Taking a pass above his head he stepped inside twice to create his own space and score what looked, for all the world, like the winning try. Both of Adams' starring turns highlighted what an absolute natural wing threequarter he is, and our thoughts went back to Pivac's 'bold' selection against Ireland when Adams was put in the centre.

'The key,' Siôn observed archly, 'is to get Adams the ball, not to move him to where the ball is.'

And here, with eight minutes to go and a six-point lead, is where you find out how well a squad has been prepared for test rugby. Throughout the game, the cameras had turned on the Welsh coaches: Pivac supporting an inscrutable smirk, and Stephen Jones holding his head in his hands. Relief must have been palpable up there as Adams was named man of the match and all that remained was to offer commiserations to the plucky Italians before skedaddling off for a break away from all those endless questions about selection and Shaun *blydi* Edwards.

So, when Ange Capuozzo turned the Welsh defence inside out in the last play of the game and handed Italy victory, it was hard not to feel some sympathy for the Wales coaching team. Hard, but not impossible, and Pivac's passionless management-speak in the post-match interview certainly smoothed my path.[1]

---

[1] Modern sports psychology demands that all disasters are viewed as educational. Wayne Pivac's insistence that 'important learnings' had been taken from scenarios like this one became too much for me over the course of the campaign. Stop learning and start crying!

'I'm off to join the queue of men punching the wall,' Siôn advised.

Driving down Newport Road as I came home to Cardiff at sunset, a few fans were still straggling up it, their scarves and jerseys hanging off them like shrouds. They deserve better than this, and so do the players.

Hatt Mancock

13 Nov 2022

'Grimacing Aneurin Bevan retches as he is forced to eat camel penis, sheep vagina, and cow's anus during gruesome *I'm a Celebrity* eating trial', would have made a startling *Daily Mail* headline in the 1940s. Substitute 'Matt Hancock' for Nye and my interest wasn't even piqued enough to watch. So jaded have I become with the tawdry lightweights that populate Westminster, I translated the headline to: 'Grubby Little Man Does Grubby Little Thing' and carried on with my day.

It's 25 years since William Hague was accused of demeaning the office of Leader of the Opposition because he allowed himself to be photographed wearing a baseball cap on a log flume. Tellingly, as it turned out, he was pictured at the *top* of the log flume, having innocently chugged up there from a world that still knew shame.

Was the fall of Rome like this? Were underpaid Centurions further burdened with tedious news of Nero's exploits in the vomitorium when all they wanted to know was whether they could afford the bill for the underfloor heating they now regretted inventing?

Dismally, much of the press has contrived to confect a moral debate over whether the TV show is the right setting for the former Secretary of State for Health to issue an apology to the nation for his conduct during the worst pandemic since the Spanish flu. How awry does your compass need to have gone if you are even considering the possibility that Boy George might be an appropriate confessor for everything that went on during Mr Hancock's stewardship of a national tragedy?

As he munches his way to four hundred grand, it will be interesting to see what thoughts Hancock has about the planned nurses' strike. If you are encumbered with friends or relatives who are blanching at the nurses' 17% pay demand, I can recommend a jolly little game where you get to adopt the crass, reductive stance so beloved of Tories and turn it back on them.

'17% is ridiculous, the country can't afford it.'

'You believe in the free market, right?'

'Yes, I have Milton Friedman's face tattooed on all my children's arms.'

'Well, there's a shortage of 40 000 nurses. What happens to the price of something when it's in short supply?'

'Oh.'

'Oh, indeed.'

You can further twist the knife thusly…

'But there might be a way to make up the shortage quickly…'

'I knew it, the free market never advantages public sector workers!'

'Yes, all you have to do is reverse your immigration rules.'

'D'oh!'

There, in a nutshell, is the hypocrisy of Brexit orthodoxy laid bare. Subtracting thousands of overseas workers would, we were told, cause wages to rise. Now, here we are in that exact scenario and anybody wanting a higher wage is accused of fuelling inflation.

'Our NHS' was the supposed beneficiary of a process that has seen it stripped of its overseas workforce whilst those remaining watch both major parties deny the market reality of their pay demand.

The NHS that was plastered on Boris Johnson's bus is purely conceptual. Like Paddington Bear or James Bond, it exists as an emotional touchstone to be invoked whenever it is expedient to manipulate the electorate. The actual NHS, as experienced by those who work in it or are treated by it, is as remote from what they had us banging pots for as performative memorialising at the Cenotaph is from a Flanders trench.

As people wait for days in A&E departments and are advised to take taxis rather than wait for ambulances, we must be clear-eyed about who is responsible for their suffering. The usual suspects will be wheeled out – the Civil Service, NHS managers, diversity programmes etc. – all taking a ritual shellacking from those with a vested interest in defending the state of the UK as it stands. Historically, nurses have been immune to direct criticism from government, owing to the respect they command amongst the electorate. We used to say that about miners, though, and a little government disinformation goes a long way.

Enjoy the spectacle of Hancock eating the nether regions of exotic animals in the jungle. Forcing him to do it via public vote is the nearest thing we have to accountability.[1]

---

[1] Tellingly, all of the criticism of this article was from people who felt it was too sympathetic to the libidinous former Secretary of State for Health.

The Red-Haired Man

29 Nov 2022

Who amongst us could have failed to be moved by FIFA president, Gianni Infantino's moving evocation of the oppression he suffered as a child on account of his now absent red hair? The infant Infantino must have been a uniquely resilient character, rising as he did from degradations that were apparently comparable to the plight of the disabled, LGBTQ people in Qatar, and exploited migrant workers, to head up an organisation so respected in world affairs that the BBC strapline for his address was: 'FIFA president condemns hypocrisy of the West.'

FIFA has spoken and West is not best, *bois bach*.

It is for we hypocritical Westerners to examine our consciences as we arrogantly point the finger at Qatari customs to which fans must conform during the World Cup.

As Infantino explained,

'If somebody has to go without a beer for three hours, he will survive.'

It's a powerful moral point. Are we really unwilling to respect the deeply held religious convictions of the host nation for a mere three hours simply to satisfy our thirst for intoxication? Shame on the West!

If you're not feeling guilty yet, then consider the lengths to which the Qataris have gone to accommodate our godless proclivities. For a mere $950, fans can quaff away to their hearts' content in a 'temporary hospitality space located in the festive hospitality village within the stadium security perimeter.'

Imagine the cost of building a temporary hospitality space

that is invisible to an omniscient god. I think you'll agree that $950 to experience such a phenomenon is more than reasonable.

Infantini's expression betrayed the deep disappointment and embarrassment he felt that, once again, it had fallen to FIFA to lead the way as regards ethical relations between the world's contrasting cultures.

When the Gulf state threw its hat into the ring to host the world's most popular winter game at the height of summer, FIFA must have been daunted by the challenge of mounting a competition that would showcase the world's spirit of cooperation as beautifully as its predecessor in Vladimir Putin's Russia.

It takes an organisation of unique vision to look at a fabulously wealthy country with no footballing history, notable players, nor stadia and see that its groundbreaking approach to employment law would allow it to become the focus of footballing dreams in record time.

So, it is not surprising that the FIFA supremo should feel moved to express his organisation's distress at criticism from a hemisphere of the world that, frankly, has no business impugning the integrity of agreements made between themselves and the eye-wateringly wealthy Qatari state.

After all, if somebody has to refrain from being gay for a month, they will survive.

The Red-Haired Man

There was a red-haired man who had no eyes or ears.
Neither did he have any hair, so he was called red-haired
theoretically.

He couldn't speak, since he didn't have a mouth. Neither did he
have a nose.

He didn't even have any arms or legs. He had no stomach and
he had no back and he had no spine and he had no innards
whatsoever. He had nothing at all!

Therefore there's no knowing whom we are even talking about.
In fact it's better that we don't say any more about him.

Daniil Ivanovich Kharms

(1905-1942)

Morning Constitutional

27 November 2022

William Windsor must be fuming, sat at home in his Abercwmboi & Fitch T-shirt[1], prevented from cheering on the nation of which he's the actual Prince, on account of holding a meaningless position as head of the English FA. All his butties texting him from Qatar:

'Where you to?'

'*Yma o hyd.*'

'?'

'In Windsor.'

The World Cup draw was bound to expose yet more cowboy structural work in what passes for the UK constitution, as notions of loyalty and nationhood are played out on the pitch in front of us. Appointing his son as Prince of Wales was King Charles' first act as monarch; in reality, it is likely the only meaningful constitutional decision he will ever take as he faces a lifetime's grimacing at all the legislative nonsense that he has to nod through without comment.

Royalty sits painfully atop a pyramid of dishonesty that claims to include the national consciousness of the Celtic nations, whilst denying their inhabitants any means to express this in the political sphere. You are free to sing Daffydd Iwan songs in your bucket hat, and look! Prince William is pretending not to support England as a symbol of that freedom. The moment the sport is over, however, your Welshness must be packed away, in case you

---

[1] These are actually available from Bagsy (bagsybags.com).

try to use it to raise taxes or decriminalise drugs. Being Welsh is fine as a hobby, even royalty likes to try its hand at the anthem, but actual, grown-up nationality belongs to the United Kingdom of Great Britain & Northern Ireland. For proof, check out your new blue passport.

Away from the roleplay of sport, the Supreme Court this week laid bare the despotic nature of intranational politics in the UK. The creation of an American-style constitutional court in the UK was always fraught with danger for those wedded to the status quo. Criticise the USA all you like for ignoring its constitution, but the document itself is a wonder of the Enlightenment: the desire for personal liberty codified in defiance of all other concerns. The UK's unwritten constitution, on the other hand, is so malleable and vague that it can be successfully tampered with by people whose intellectual ballast wouldn't ground a moth. *Dominic Raab has entered the chat*.

So, creating a body of eminent lawyers to scrutinise the workings of the Heath Robinson mechanism of UK governance was bound to expose its incompetence and iniquity for all to see. The court is charged with applying reason to the accumulated traditions and habits that the UK has used and abused to get its business done. The scales of justice are an inadequate metaphor, as the constitution has previously trundled on without the counterweight of any public scrutiny. The Supreme Court is more akin to a brutally honest speak-your-weight machine. Ask it a question and the bald truth emerges.

'What constitutional grounds did Boris Johnson have to prorogue parliament?'

'None, he did it entirely illegally and had Jacob Rees-Mogg lie to the queen about it.'

'Okay, by what constitutional mechanism can the people of Scotland trigger a referendum on independence?'

'No such mechanism exists; the people of Scotland have no

111

democratic route to self-determination at all.'

In the final, desperate days of the Scottish referendum campaign, the UK government, with the help of Gordon Brown, made 19 promises to the Scottish electorate in a successful bid to trade enhanced devolution for continuance of the UK. Furthermore, it was put to the Scottish people that a vote to remain in the UK was the surest way of guaranteeing Scotland's membership of the European Union. All 19 promises have been broken and, you may have noticed, Scotland is no longer a member of the EU.

In any other contractual agreement, such behaviour would result in severance and a requirement for damages to be paid. Contracts, however, require consideration on either side, and the Supreme Court made it clear this week that there is nothing contractual about Scotland's relationship to the UK. Rather, Scotland is wholly subsumed by a union that devolves powers as privileges, not rights.

It was jarring to see *The Sun* newspaper on sale in our capital city on Saturday morning. The front-page referencing Friday's game[2]: 'At least we're on the brink of going through...'

One can only assume that is the royal 'we'.

---

[2] The English football team had played.

Don't Mention the Culture War

4 December 2022

'Daddy, what did you do in the Culture War?'

'I posted a meme of the Duchess of Sussex with Prince Harry on a lead but those were dark times, son. Never speak of them again.'

In the olden days you used to know when you were in a war because Tony Blair would start acting even more like a double-glazing salesman than usual. With a flash of the demonic grin that seduced a nation in 1997, Middle Eastern cities would be reduced to rubble and *The Sun* would rush out an 'Our Boys in the Gulf' commemorative edition featuring Linda Lusardi in a khaki bikini.

The actual fighting of the war tended to be left to professional servicemen and the unfortunate residents of wherever we were liberating. Our job, as armchair liberators, was to watch guided missiles blow up flat-roofed buildings on the news and then purchase computer games based on the conflict.

Your modern vicarious warrior, on the other hand, is a far more sophisticated consumer of warfare. Nowadays, we demand to be part of the action ourselves and lay our enemies to waste on social media as we fight for noble causes that permit neither nuance nor negotiation. It's do or die on Twitter for cultural warriors and, make no mistake, they must be taken *seriously*, or you'll be unfriended at the very least.

At any given moment, battalions of our fellow citizens are valiantly calling each other names in the service of concepts that define the very soul of humanity. Uncle Keith is fighting for freedom of speech during the ad break; Mum is defending biological womanhood for a couple of hours because her Pilates class has been cancelled; your daughter has put off her GCSE revision to decolonise the Llantwit Major community Facebook page, and your window cleaner hosts a YouTube channel devoted to unmasking the machinations of the World Economic Forum.

The common factor in all the arguments that comprise the culture war is that they are insoluble. At no point are trans people going to agree to stop being quite so trans, nor are their opponents about to suggest they be allowed to self-identify but only on Mondays and Wednesdays.

Such an argument must be distressing and exhausting for those whose lives are intrinsically affected by the issue. These people, however, comprise a tiny minority of those engaged with the debate, and this is the defining feature of all culture war activity: it is a risk-free sport for those who have no skin in the game, whilst being potentially devastating for those who do.

When our leisure time was spent meeting each other in person, it was considered impolite to discuss politics and religion unless they were the reason everyone was there. Nobody wanted the hassle. Now, as public spaces are diminishing by the day and social media fills the gap, ideological strife has become an unavoidable part of daily life for many of us.

In a functioning democracy, the facility for everyone to debate issues of the day would be a great development. From it, new ideas could emerge, and meaningful political movements could be forged. Far from democratising society, however, the internet seems to have hived off debate into a meaningless free-for-all and provided an illusion of solidarity for participants who, in reality, are growing ever more isolated and vulnerable to manipulation.

The terms of the debate are directed with ruthless efficiency by those with control over the flow of information. So, this week people are lined up behind either Lady Susan Hussey or Ngozi Fulani, neither of whom anybody recognised until last week, in a dispute over a conversation nobody heard at an unremarkable palace reception. Once engaged with the debate, people are cornered by algorithms that show them the opinions they want to see.[1] We are persuaded that the trivial is noteworthy and then set upon each other to fight for opinions which have been fed to us by our handlers.

Freedom of expression has replaced religion as the opium of the masses. As our standard of living declines, we are wasting ourselves in parlour games that serve no function but to perpetuate themselves and exhaust our capacity to protest. The culture war is *Eastenders* for the self-important.

---

[1] No need to thank your tech correspondent for this cutting-edge explanation, all in a day's work.

More at Stake

Having to hunt around the TV schedules to find where to watch the game has added a new layer of desperation to an already uncomfortable experience. This time, it appears that Sky Sports have acquired the rights to monetise our misery which, for me, precludes even the dignity of a private viewing at home. No, I shall watch Wales play South Africa today in the pub, alongside fellow wretched souls, compelled as we are by tribal loyalty and the distant memories of better times, to subject ourselves to the masochism of hope in the face of reason.

It's fair to say that the match in Pretoria is not at the forefront of the national conversation. Perhaps life outside the goldfish bowl might benefit a team that boasts more talent than their Six Nations performances suggest. Wayne Pivac has spoken of sleepless nights since the loss to Italy and we must hope that he has spent them coming up with a coherent idea of who plays where and why. One of his favourite phrases is 'taking learnings' from games.[1] One of the learnings he needs to have taken is that test matches are not often won by the sort of grand gamble that saw him play Josh Adams in the centre against Ireland. Even at the time that smacked of the type of desperation that takes hold when preparation has been inadequate.

We are at one of those junctures in the team's fortunes where most of us would accept a losing performance as long as it suggested clarity of purpose. I doubt many of us expect a series victory in South Africa, but we do need to see a path

---

[1] Get over it, Ben.

forward that makes some kind of sense.

Because, let's be frank, particularly for those of us who carry the trauma of the early 90s like a war wound, these have been a grim few months for the faithful. Even before the loss to Italy, the Principality Stadium seemed to be hosting the fall of a civilisation, with the WRU obliged to water down the beer amidst tales of drunken degradation and 'fans' paying £100 only to ignore the game.[2]

An identity crisis continues to grip the regional scene, which increasingly resembles a branding exercise on *The Apprentice*. It would be a welcome development if those running rugby in Cardiff and Newport would acknowledge that the names of their clubs are not the number one priority of those who might be persuaded to go and see them play. 'Pleeeeease Dad, can we go and see the Goldie Lookin Dragons play Capital Elite RFC at Rodney Parade?'

It has been fashionable, of late, to consign rugby to Welsh cultural history. That bloke who has strung a washing line off the side of the Rhigos[3] exhorted the Welsh Affairs Committee to, 'get away from sheep, wet weather and... rugby' in favour of promoting, you've guessed it, 'adventure tourism'. Perhaps he could demonstrate his commitment to risk-based leisure activities by expounding this view at half-time in a rugby club of his choice this afternoon?

Over all of this hangs the loss to the game, and the nation, of Phil Bennett who personified the sheer joy that rugby in Wales has brought to us and the world. He was, of course, also a fine soccer player and it has been saddening to see some commentators trying to fabricate division between fans of the

---

[2] Each game during this period seemed to produce reports of a first-match-attending child being vomited upon from above by drunken revellers. It's difficult to summon elegiac prose from material like that.

[3] A new zipwire attraction that I am precluded from enjoying because I am big-boned.

117

two games when success at either is a source of pride for the overwhelming majority of us. It is a fact, though, that the children of Wales will be finding inspiration in our football team this autumn that isn't currently on offer from their rugby counterparts.

So, there is more than a result at stake today for our national side. With expectations low, we need them to demonstrate that rugby deserves its place in our imagination. A respectable performance at altitude against the world champions would halt a narrative that serves only those who either dislike the game or profit from sensationalising its difficulties. I'll find a perch and hope that the boys shut them up. *Yma o hyd.*

Thick as Mince

18 Dec 2022

I've been stuck in with Covid this week so Mrs W, who has a less serious variant[1], is being treated to my insights into current affairs on a 24/7 basis. The combination of a high fever and a Twitter addiction can produce a fugue state that reaches shamanic proportions with the addition of a little gin, so it's been nice to offer her a prolonged glimpse of the passionate, socially alert rhetoric that drew her to me in the first place.

'Perhaps this would be better saved for your column,' she sometimes sniffles. And that's the kind of woman she is – always thinking of what's best for me, even if it impinges on our precious time together. Today, bless her, she's put her earphones in to watch a film, so I won't be disturbed while writing. Happy Christmas, honey!

Being at home on Twitter is, I can confirm from personal experience, much the same as being at home on drugs. You spend long periods of time talking bollocks to people you shouldn't have invited round whilst neglecting personal hygiene and spiritual wellbeing.

Recently, of course, the Trainspottingesque experience has been enlivened by the arrival of Begbie, in the shape of Elon Musk, plonking himself down on the fag-burned sofa and menacingly insisting that he's your mate. You'll be halfway through telling Piers Morgan he's a cocaine-addled gerbil with an inferiority complex and Elon will crash into your feed to

---

[1] This was the first of many appearances for Mrs W. For the purposes of the column, she's brighter than me and resigned to tolerating my obsessive political belligerence. What do publishers always advise? 'Write what you know.'

announce he's banning adverbs because they inhibit the vigour of sentences. It can only be a matter of time before he installs himself on Tesla's satnav system and prohibits left turns.

There are people whose presence on Twitter is suspiciously ubiquitous. In the past, these tended to be *golly-gosh-the-Tories-are-a-bit-rum* style stand-up wannabees whose pro-EU, middle-class simperings greased through the algorithm to win Centrist hearts. Tweeters like 'Supertanskiii' and 'Russ in Cheshire' are wholly unknown outside of the app but were so pervasive on it that criticising them was to risk evisceration by thousands of radicalised Waitrose customers.

Times change, and with them, the algorithm. In its Muskovite version, there's no longer much scope for tepid liberals to smarm their way to Patreon incomes and spots on panel shows. Nowadays, I find my feed flooded with the musings of GB News presenters and fringe Tory politicians. Prominent amongst the former are Darren Grimes and Sophie Corcoran. If you haven't had the pleasure, Darren is a spindly young man from the North-East of England who first showed up as a cause célèbre for Brexiteers when his activities for pro-Brexit group BeLeave were investigated by the Electoral Commission. Since then, he has carved himself out a niche as the voice of working-class Brexiteers who feel disenfranchised in a UK where the last three Prime Ministers have been rabid Brexit supporters, and in which His Majesty's Opposition concur. Until a couple of weeks ago when it was cancelled[2], he had a GB News show called *Real Britain* on which he poses as a mouthpiece for the views of 'ordinary' Britons who are repulsed by the unpatriotic, woke agenda of the BBC, Sky, and the RNLI.

The title of his show is interesting, I think, and bears some analysis. It's possible that Darren hasn't had time to read Ece Temelkuran's terrifying book *How to Lose a Country* on the methods Recep Tayyip Erdogan uses to nullify educated

---

[2] Since reinstated.

opposition to his agenda, but prime amongst them is instilling the notion that considered opinions are less authentic than visceral reactions. From there, it is simple to project that anybody who holds considered opinions is less genuine than those who rely on gut reaction to form their views and, before you know it, you have a large segment of the population believing that their ignorance is a signifier of authenticity. Do you live in Real Britain? Not if you're this far into an article you don't, so relax and have a soy latte.

The coming star of right-wing Twittery, however, is Sophie Corcoran; a Durham University student who has parlayed her Twitter game into a media presence that saw her interviewed about Meghan Markle on US news this week. Sophie appears to tweet everything that occurs to her during her waking hours, including some things for which she wakes up specifically. Like Darren, she is at pains to emphasise her working-class credentials, never more so than when explaining that trades unions are betraying working people by asking for them to be paid more.

'Mick Lynch is rattled – he knows he's finally lost all support and that the public know this is about bringing down the govt, not T&Cs.'

Her relentless political commentary is interspersed with breezy chit-chat that sometimes seems at odds with the wide-ranging command of complex issues she evinces otherwise.

'I have today learnt that mince pies don't actually have mince (like spag bol mince) in it. I've always wondered how people eat them cold.'

Certainly, there is a peculiar cohesion to the political messaging put forward by Darren, Sophie, and a host of others who are connected either to GB News or the think tanks that operate from Tufton Street in London. A cynic might infer that their pronouncements, rather than being the authentic expression of British youth, were being coordinated centrally.

121

In terms of engagement, though, these people are smashing it out of the park on social media, to the point where they are unavoidable. Indeed, their style has been adopted by the fustier voices we are more used to hearing promote the same ideas. Here is John Redwood, who, you might remember, was recently in the frame to be Liz Truss's Chancellor.

'We hear how the NHS is short of beds. Why don't managers put more in?'

You need to be more *authentic* John, like when you sang the Welsh anthem.

In 1997, when I was also a spindly young man, my university lecturer, Professor Pete McLeay, used to rail at us that the age of information was coming, and we needed to be very alert to who owned the means of transmission. A change of ownership can have peculiar effects.

If you'll excuse me, Mrs W has removed her headphones and I am keen to have a chat with her about the unusually small turnout in the Tunisian Parliamentary elections.

A Right, Royal Pain

26 Dec 2022

A glance at my previous columns will reveal my feelings about royalty so don't @ me, but Chazza's first bash at a Christmas speech seemed well judged to me. Striking a contemplative tone, the novice monarch managed to touch on a number of issues that unify us at this time of year, and interestingly without ignoring the desperate state of the nation.

The remaining acceptable royals – Camilla, William, Kate, Edward, Sophie, and Anne were shown off in a predictably Disneyfied montage of caring activities to illustrate Charles' central theme of public service. Andrew, Harry, and Meghan have, of course, been airbrushed out of the picture Soviet-style, and it was rictus grins and empathy frowns all round for the remaining cast as they engaged with the great unwashed for the cameras.

In his first address to the nation, the day after his mother's passing, Charles was at pains to emphasise that his days as a gobby critic of the body politic were at an end now that he had assumed the throne. In that same speech, however, he unnecessarily installed William as Prince of Wales, completely evading any political scrutiny as even Plaid Cymru felt too inhibited by the etiquette of mourning to object. Since then, he's kept his hand in politically by using sarcasm to provide a thin cloak of deniability, notably dissing Sir Jeffrey Donaldson of the DUP whilst casting the royal glow of approval over Sinn Fein's Michelle O'Neill.

And this is the thing with Charles: he's a complicated man. Given that the DUP's *raison d'être* is loyalty to the Crown, you might expect Charles to favour them over the organisation whose armed wing assassinated his uncle. Whatever was going on during that meeting, it seems to have come as a surprise to all involved except the lad himself.

The Christmas message had a hint of subversion, too, if you cared to look. On the surface, Charles' message was about unity and service. These are the touchstones of the modern royal schtick and the favoured tropes for justifying their continuance in national life. So far, so Elizabethan. It didn't take him long to put his own stamp on proceedings, however. Having related his experience in Bethlehem to underscore his own faith, he named other religions as the equal of his own and explicitly extended his message to include those of no faith. He characterised Christmas as a celebration of light overtaking darkness which, as anybody with a Jethro Tull album knows, is a decidedly Pagan interpretation of the festival. For years, Charles has said that he intended to be a defender of the *faiths* and on his first yuletide outing, he seems to have come good on that ambition.

Whilst the section on service fulfilled a clunky PR role for the slimmed-down Firm, it also featured an extended tribute to public service workers. The armed forces were mentioned first, but extremely briefly and that, of itself, drew a distinction with the Duke of Edinburgh's directorial choice to place Her Maj between tanks like a cross between Rambo and your nan.

Charles' vision of service extended to the NHS and care workers. Interestingly, footage of ambulances was used to illustrate this and it's difficult to believe that the palace was unaware of the contention this might provoke during the current disputes. As he paid tribute to 'health and social care professionals, our teachers and indeed all those working in public service, whose skill and commitment are at the heart of our communities' one could imagine the consternation in Downing Street.

Charles, it seems, is going to be a handful. As public sector disputes spread in the New Year we will doubtless see government rhetoric intensifying as the Tory administration seeks to discredit the strikers, calling into question their patriotism and wider motives. Despite polls showing 70% public support for the strikes, Keir Starmer's opposition is committed to treading an imaginary middle line which they are convinced will win over floating voters.

So far, the only ringing endorsement of public sector workers has come from a king who seems to believe that he is one himself. He has positioned himself as an embarrassment to the right, who profess loyalty but disagree with everything he says, and the left who agree with his positions but believe in the abolition of his role. For politicians, Charles looks set to be a right, royal pain.[1]

---

[1] Voluntarily written and filed on Christmas Day in an 'apple for teacher' bid to gain favour over rival columnists.

The Deeds to Our Souls

3 July 2022

I had my hope levels set as close to zero as possible for this one. Having spent the Six Nations travelling around Wales reporting on regional variations of despair, today's perch was close to home at the Colliers Arms in Porth. A respectable crowd had gathered for the game, with a few jerseys on show, but the mood was subdued as we braced ourselves for the worst.

With actual Zulu warriors heralding the arrival of the Springboks, and a lone voice committing GBH to '*Hen Wlad Fy Nhadau*', older viewers were wondering if Stanley Baker would be making an appearance.

Glancing at Twitter, the South African fans were in bullish humour.

'The Welsh look like lambs to the slaughter,' tweeted Nqaba Magwa.

'That aged well,' I replied two minutes later, as Louis Rees-Zammit put us into the lead.

'Guests first,' quipped Nqaba with a cheeky smiley.[1]

And we were off on one of those test match afternoons that knocks years off your life-expectancy but reminds you that however badly it has let you down, wasted your money and abused your trusting nature, the WRU has a lockbox on Westgate Street that contains the deeds to your soul.

---

[1] It was lovely sending this article to Nqaba. I didn't know him at all, it was the digital equivalent of the sort of banter we have with opposing fans in the pub. He was amazed to find himself in the Welsh press. I know how he feels.

With the 'Boks seeming rusty and lacking in cohesion, Wales were alert to their fumbles and when Rees-Zammit pounced on one to put us further ahead there were glances of disbelief around the Colliers' lounge.

18-3 up at half-time, some of us were beginning to feel we might have been a tad over-critical of the current set-up of late.

A seasoned campaigner at the next table, Gando, confided,

'To be honest, I thought they'd be lining up the body bags for us out there.'

I sympathised with him. At least he hadn't said it in print, as recently as that morning.

Somewhere, in a parallel universe, Wales going in 15 points up at half-time means that we can relish the prospect of the second half. In this corner of the cosmos, however, there is an immutable law that dictates the first 10 minutes after the break must be spent in rapt trauma as our lead is frittered away. Every last one of us knew what was coming and it was met not with outrage, but muted murmurings that confirmed the inevitability of a South African revival.

Gando didn't comment. He just turned to me with the hollow look of a man whose lot is to endure this for life. I nodded.

But this Welsh side seems to be taking on the characteristics of its captain. Dan Biggar is not the sort of flawless Captain Marvel in whose wake a team becomes more efficient by default. His on-field demeanour puts you in mind of the sort of bloke whose antics cause you to be dragged into a fight outside a nightclub when you'd gone out for a quiet curry. He speaks to referees as if they were traffic wardens and is prone to occasional errors that tend to be sensational in scope. Crucially, though, he is possessed of a fighting spirit usually associated with the kind of dog it's illegal to own nowadays.

So, when Wales were trailing the world champions, at

altitude, with their best scrummager carried off senseless and being refereed by a man who had won the job in the Georgian national lottery, Biggar's team looked positively energised. They went down to 14, 13, and finally 12 men without losing an ounce of competitive intensity.

Now we were hooked. In the last 10 minutes, the Colliers finally found its voice and the familiar music of gasps, groans and ferchristssakesmuns rang out into the lower Rhondda. It was cruel at the end, particularly that Biggar should have been penalised personally for South Africa's winning kick, but Welsh rugby won something back yesterday that it was in danger of losing. Yes, South Africa were poor, no, we're still not reliably physical enough up front, but this Wales side can play a full role in the drama of the world game. Nobody should be breaking into the WRU's lockbox just yet.

'Tis the Season to Be Angry

1 Jan 2023

The late Pope Benedict was described on Saturday as a 'doctrinal enforcer' and that is very much how I see my role here at *Nation.Cymru*, and, indeed, in life generally. So, whilst I accept that many of you may be suffering the effects of last night's frivolities, I must urge you to set aside your indulgences and refocus upon the rotting corpse of the body politic.

The tone of walking platitude Rishi Sunak's New Year message suggested a stranger who had knocked on your door mid-party to explain that he'd run over your dog.

'Hi everybody…' the PM began, affecting his best corporate-casual bounce. What followed was less 'Happy New Year' than 'You have my deepest sympathy'. The gist was:

- Things have been bloody awful.
- It's all Putin's fault.
- Everything the government has done was for your own good.
- Ukraine
- Ukraine
- Ukraine
- 2023 will be worse but you get a day off for the Coronation.

Squinting through a hangover at your dying Christmas tree, you'd be forgiven for replacing Bing Crosby with Leonard Cohen and heading for the potting shed with your service revolver.

But no! I exhort you, dear reader, to rise from your slough of despond and hear the clarion call of rebellion. Are we really, after

129

12 years of *Carry on Torying*, just going to let them shrug and tell us that's the best they can do?

Here's a couple of recent developments to fire you up a bit.

You might have noticed that there's a spot of industrial unrest going around at the moment. I think I've touched on it once or twice here. Well, in *The Times* this week, a 'government source' divulged the strategy that Downing Street has come up with to resolve the strikes that are paralysing Britain. They have, apparently, calculated that the unions will run out of money in April so intend to negotiate in bad faith until then in the belief that the strikes will collapse. To put it another way: our elected government is willing to see its citizens deprived of healthcare, transport, education, post, and administration until its public sector workers are forced to accept pay cuts. No attempt to resolve the issues will be made, this is a zero-sum game that pits the private sector against the public to the detriment of both. Plan B, presumably, is to accuse postmen of eating the Easter Bunny.

Meanwhile, *The Telegraph*, which caters to the barmier end of bewildered Boris fans, seized upon Mark Drakeford's resignation timetable to call for an end to devolution. Now, call me old-fashioned, but I was given to understand that the approved route to changing policy was by voting for something different; not by abolishing democracy altogether and handing power to another body. Got to be a bit awks for Andrew RT Davies at Conservative Central Office.[1]

'So, what's the plan to make sure I romp to victory and become First Minister?'

'About that, dear boy, polling suggests that we can win an extra 13 votes in Tunbridge Wells by abolishing the Senedd so if you could carry on exactly as you are now that'd be a real help.'

'Oh.'

---

[1] He is NOT a figment of my imagination. Seriously, look him up; he's got a Twitter page and everything.

Do you see a pattern emerging here? The Tories have managed three prime ministers in six months, without troubling the electorate for a mandate, whilst admitting that the UK is in a parlous state and set to deteriorate further. If anybody expresses displeasure through the ballot box, they threaten to take it away, and those who protest at work face being starved out and vilified to the wider public. The message is: even we know we are useless, but you are stuck with us and there is nothing you can do about it.

As you hoover up the pine needles, take a moment to reflect on Baroness Mone on her yacht with Ultimo bras stuffed full of your cash, or of ex-Tory Chairman Jake Berry telling us that the way to deal with the cost-of-living crisis was to 'get a better job', or of Gavin Williamson becoming Sir Gavin Williamson.

The mince pies are finished, the gas bills are coming, and it's time to get even. *Bonne chance, mes braves,* may the New Year bring what you deserve.

Mate

8 Jan 2023

Wandering round Barry Island on Bank Holiday Monday, I passed one of those modern fathers that they have nowadays refusing a request from his small son.

'I'm not sure, we'll have to wait until Mum gets back, mate.'

A better version of me would have stopped and explained to the child that his father's use of the word 'mate' was the choice of a morally weak man who was attempting to impose his will whilst avoiding accountability for his decision. As the outing was a special treat for Mrs W, however, I abrogated my civic duty and remained outwardly cheerful as we pressed on to the chip shop.

The godfather of this sort of oleaginous shithousery is, of course, Tony 'I think most people recognise I'm a pretty straightforward guy' Blair. In 1997, power-hungry narcissists the world over looked on in awe as he groomed the UK with ladles of hopey-changey gloop that belied his ultimate legacy as the man who hollowed out the country into a corporate shell while setting fire to the Middle East.

Key to Blair's success was the tone of voice he adopted when giving speeches. Looking upwards, as if at the shining sun of a new dawn, he would beseech the electorate using a rising pitch that landed just short of pleading. After 12 years of Margaret Thatcher barking at us, followed by John Major's defeated whimperings, the nation was ready to be *appealed* to. The effect was to suggest that not only was change possible, but that we could be part of it.

This, presumably, is the tonal range that Rishi Sunak was aiming for in his relaunch speech this week. Sunak, though, is beguiling nobody. During the Blair years there was concern that politics was emphasising style over substance, with presentational technique obscuring a threadbare ideological landscape. Sunak's offer comprises no ideology at all and presentation more suited to a shopping channel at the far end of the Freeview listings.

The guiding principle of his approach is that you and I are thicker than a whale omelette. Consequently, we need to have simple phrases repeated to us *over and over again* in case they fall through the holes in our tiny, proletarian minds. Hammering home a slogan is nothing new; by the time of the 1997 election my dog used to say, 'Tough on crime, tough on the causes of crime,' if he wanted a biscuit. He got one too, because he'd demonstrated an enlightened approach to law and order, which signalled an openness to progressive social policy whilst acknowledging the rights of victims. Good dog, Max.

Sunak, on the other hand, chose relentless repetition of the phrase 'our children and grandchildren' as a motif for his speech. The rationale for this was unclear, but might have been to suggest that the slider-wearing plutocrat was 'one of us' in so much as he possesses the requisite human qualities to procreate. Alternatively, he might have been indicating that the fruits of his policies would be reaped by future generations and encouraging us to relinquish the last vestiges of our own hopes for contentment. Either way, it epitomised the terminal vacuity at the heart of his speech and, by extension, his government. The PM's theme was 'the people's priorities', of which there were five.

Whenever a politician invokes 'the people' my hackles raise as I am bound to hear about a homogenous blob of humanity that is 'hard-working', 'decent' and happens to agree with everything they say. This time 'the people' were treated to a Derren-Brown-style demonstration of psychic showmanship as Sunak revealed to us what we wanted him to do.

'Think of a government priority, any priority, don't tell me what it is. Is it halving inflation?'

133

'The spirits are speaking now. I'm getting the word…migrants.'

The 'people's priorities' turn out to be the exact same things that the government was already going to do. I mean, what are the odds?

The likelihood is that this Westminster government is toast regardless of what it does between now and an election. Sunak spoke of 'restoring trust in politics' whilst mounting a specious political stunt that insulted the intelligence of anybody that witnessed it. The sense of impending disaster is palpable on these islands and people are losing their lives as our essential services crumble before our eyes. So, don't talk to us of trust. We have been lied to, gaslit and swindled for as long as any of us can remember. The 'people's priority' is that you and everybody like you be removed from influence over our lives.

Is that clear, mate?

The Real Ting

15 Jan 2023

When Communism fell, news reached us from the formerly sealed off nation of Albania that Norman Wisdom was its most popular film star. In fact, he was Albania's only Western celebrity – his films, uniquely, had been approved by Enver Hoxha as being ideologically pure enough for consumption by the Albanian masses. For Hoxha, a brutal dictator who prohibited beards and saxophones, Wisdom's screen persona of a pratfalling, downtrodden simpleton forever in conflict with his overbearing boss symbolised the Albanian people's struggle against Western imperialism. Wisdom was unaware of the iconic status that daily showings of his films on state TV had bestowed upon him until the regime fell and emigres started arriving in the West. In 1995, when his career was largely over in the UK, Wisdom visited Albania and was mobbed by delirious fans.

This closely mirrors the experience of Welsh Conservative leader Andrew 'Real Ting' Davies, a largely ignored figure here in Wales, who commands huge popularity amongst Conservative members in England. In the latest ConservativeHome survey, they rate Mr Davies 11 points higher than the Prime Minister, Rishi Sunak. He outpoints Nadhim Zahawi, Michael Gove, Dominic Raab, Thérèse Coffey, Grant Shapps, Jeremy Hunt, Robert Jenrick, and David TC Davies although, to be fair, several of the sub-lineages of the Omicron BA.5 variant of Covid-19 received more Christmas cards than David TC Davies, whose initials unfortunately don't suggest an amusing acronym.

Psephologically minded readers will, of course, point out that the ConservativeHome survey reflects the views of an unrepresentative section of the electorate. This is true, for 12 months before her election as leader, economic hooligan Liz Truss maintained first place in the poll with unprecedented approval ratings exceeding 80 points. For Mr Davies, however, this constituency in the wider UK offers a sight more validation than his performance attracts here in Wales. His party has little to no hope of gaining power in the Senedd, so Davies has two choices as to how he approaches his role. He could provide constructive opposition from the right, emphasising private sector solutions and the potential for UK-wide cooperation. This would ensure that devolved government faced Conservative scrutiny and could, conceivably, lead to the building of consensus on some issues over time. But as David Cameron said when getting the hell out of Dodge after the Brexit vote, 'Why should I do all the hard shit?' Because committing to diligent opposition in an electoral environment that offers no hope of victory is zero fun. And the Welsh Conservative Party is all about fun.

So, Davies' favoured mode of opposition has been to lob bombs at Labour and Plaid without offering an alternative programme. This approach not only guarantees an easy life (not unlike my own) but goes down a treat with his fan club in England. This is where Davies' position is most problematic. On paper, his job is to work towards a Conservative Welsh Government. That's not going to happen, so trashing the incumbent Labour administration is a way to gain approval from the right wing of English Toryworld. These people, though, don't believe there should be a Welsh Government *at all* so Davies is collaborating in the abolition of his own position.

This brings to mind the antics of Nigel Farage *et al* who, for years, used their elected positions (not that bit, obvs, Davies is a list appointee) in the European Parliament to mock the institution for the benefit of those in the UK who sought to abandon it. Their strategy was not to engage with the Parliament but to discredit and ridicule it, often dishonestly.

Davies' Twitter profile describes him as 'Husband, father, farmer, Welsh Conservative leader'. This reassuringly traditional list of priorities is redolent of the Welsh Conservatives of old: reactionary old buffers and dears with gin blossoms and the whiff of wet dogs. What's tweeted out underneath this, however, reveals a thoroughly 2023 media operative whose tweets are calculated to inflame, divide and distract. A couple of weeks ago I wrote about right wing Twitter with reference to rent-a-gobs like Darren Grimes and Sophie Corcoran, whose inflammatory messaging is unavoidable on the platform and seemingly coordinated with others to push daily lines that mix cultural populism with hard right economic theory. The tone is of a voluble workmate who not only insists on airing their views on Meghan Markle whilst you're trying to read your emails but then moves seamlessly to conclude that we should privatise the NHS.

The Culture War works by building a disproportionately fierce consensus around trivial issues (royalty, statues, TV comedy etc.) and then mobilising that alliance behind economic causes (private medicine, anti-union legislation, tax cuts etc.). Have a look at some of Mr Davies' recent Twitter output:

'You cannot buy class.' (Accompanied by a photo of a smiling Wills & Kate).

'Strikes are putting our health, safety, and economy at risk. That's why the government is bringing in new laws to guarantee us minimum service levels. Labour should get out of the pockets of unions and on to the side of British workers.'

'Might be a coincidence, but my tweets are getting a lot more engagement since @elonmusk took over. Thanks Elon, have a great Christmas!'

'I prefer the pre-Meghan Harry.' (Crying emoji).

'Reality contestant apologises for appearing on GB News. There's nothing diverse or tolerant about this.'

It would seem that the common-sense yeoman of the land has been replaced by a hot-take scourge of the wokerati. A cynical observer might suspect that the nod to GB News suggests someone who is considering swapping the silage shed for the bright lights of an alt-right media career once his side gig in the Senedd comes to an end.

Whether Davies writes this stuff himself or pays someone to do it, there is little in his output that offers anything constructive as regards the governance of Wales. Tonally, he is sneering rather than questioning or inspiring, and that is a good indicator of how seriously he takes his prospects in Welsh politics. Sidelined to the point of irrelevance here, he seems to have calculated that an audience lies over the border, where his ideologically pure stance on Brexit guarantees him exposure.

Whether tripping over an anvil before clutching your foot and crying, 'Look at the Welsh NHS, Mr Grimsdale!' is enough to secure a career in the cut-throat world of English Tory politics or punditry remains unclear as we go to press.

Non-Sequitur

10 July 2022

When I'm writing about a game, I tend to start concocting a narrative as it goes along. Themes develop as the games unfold and they begin to suggest a couple of possible outcomes in even the most closely contested match. If the match is part of a series, then there is a second, overarching narrative that plays into this. How did the contest develop from the previous outing?

So, you'll appreciate that I'm in unknown territory here, as South Africa selected an entirely different team to contest a game that's outcome had seemingly no connection with the flow of play.

I'd tried to create a bit of continuity, myself, by watching the game in the Colliers, Porth as I had last week. Aptly, as it turned out, there seemed to be an entirely different clientele in for the game – I should have taken up *Nation.Cymru*'s offer of a first-class flight to Bloemfontein after all.[1] The first half seemed to map out the story easily. Wales are vastly improved from the Six Nations but lack the cutting edge to trouble the top sides. In contact, South Africa were clearly dominant, but Wales were prospering under the high ball, with a resurgent Alex Cuthbert using his height to great effect out wide. As soon as that thought crystalised, off he went injured, giving way to a heavily strapped Josh Adams for whom this tour had seemed a washout.

There were positives to note as the half wore on and the Welsh defence looked solid under pressure. Dan Lydiate

---

[1] Actually, I'd had a rough week at work and couldn't be bothered to fulfil my brief to venture out into the rugby heartlands and report back. The convoluted self-justification and brittle humour on show here betray guilt.

reminded us of what a destructive tackler he is when fit and, on the other side of the back row, Tommy Reffell's jackaling underlined his status as the find of the year.

In attack, however, Wales seemed to offer nothing. We all screamed that they were too deep during the Six Nations, but now they were slinging the ball frantically from side to side under the onslaught of the South African rush defence.

There hadn't been a murmur of excitement in the Collier's as the teams went in deadlocked 3-3 at half-time. It seemed inevitable that the second half would swing towards South Africa, as their physical presence opened up gaps for a backline that looked far livelier than that fielded in Pretoria.

Right enough, as the second half developed, Wales' defence began to look ever more stretched, and infringements rewarded South Africa with the lead. Virtually every passage of play seemed to be conducted whilst South Africa had a penalty advantage, so the pressure was continually on a Welsh side that managed, somehow, to minimise the damage.

Modern test rugby, however, is a 23-man game and when the replacements started to come on, they brought new possibilities with them, except for Alun Wyn Jones. It's becoming clear that he sold his soul to the devil for our 2021 Six Nations title, as every subsequent game seems to bring new agonies for our veteran hero. This time he was shown a yellow card for interfering with a ball he never so much as touched. Can we fly somebody out to perform an exorcism before the final test, please?

As the minutes ticked down, Wales began to try a more expansive approach, with Tomos Williams looking to pass. Gareth Anscombe put us within a score with a well-taken penalty before missing the next one, and it seemed inevitable that the Boks would close out the game.

In the Colliers all was quiet. Throughout the game it had

been muted with the odd applause for South African errors underscoring the anticlimactic nature of this week's game weighed next to the drama in Pretoria.

So, when Josh Adams flew over for a beautifully worked try that left us one behind, a sudden eruption of noise gave way to stunned anxiety as Anscombe teed up a difficult conversion. Even after he put it over, the final couple of minutes were heavy with the expectation that yet another infringement would see Wales lose at the death once again. Somehow, though, the Welsh scrum held firm as the clock ticked into extra time and concerted pressure forced a fumble from the home side to secure our first ever victory on South African soil.

Nothing about this result made the slightest sense. Perhaps Sir Gareth was right when he intimated that the South Africans had angered the rugby gods with their selection this week. However it happened, we go into the final test with the series alive and a side who have vastly outperformed expectations.

We are forever being implored to learn lessons from the southern hemisphere when it comes to rugby so, in the light of northern hemisphere victories today, I feel I should pay tribute to the southern hemisphere style of journalism by calling for Australia, New Zealand, South Africa and Argentina to be removed from the top table of the international game and required to qualify for the World Cup against the Pacific nations. Be sure to tweet this article at your rugby pals Down Under.

Getting Away with It

22 January 2023

'If you don't believe in God, all you have to believe in is decency. Decency is very good. Better decent than indecent. But I don't think it's enough.'

This Harold Macmillan quote should rightly enrage the principled atheist who asserts that their moral compass is efficiently calibrated by sensitivity to the plight of others and does not require a divine technician. By instinct, I agree that ethical behaviour that is motivated by obedience lacks the personal discipline required for Godless virtue. But then there is Dominic Raab.

Asked if former Chancellor and current Conservative Chair Nadhim Zahawi would still be in the party in a month's time following revelations that he paid a £1 million penalty for irregular tax declarations, Raab chuckled and observed that, 'A month is a long time in politics.'

A variation of this cynical aphorism is often attributed to Harold Wilson, but even that noted practitioner of the dark arts would surely blanch at the fetid pond in which UK politics is currently conducted. Implicit in Raab's airy dismissal of the charges against Zahawi is the assumption that these people are accountable to nobody. Rishi Sunak's second fixed penalty notice, this time for filming himself in a car without a seatbelt, was similarly waved away by the Deputy Prime Minister, for whom all transgressions are morally equal. Whether trivial or serious, all that distinguishes a wrongdoing in Raabworld is whether the wrongdoer has the political clout to ride out the accusation.

Raab, of course, has good reason to subscribe to a code of ethics last seen jotted down on Nero's Grade 3 violin book. Mired in multiple accusations of bullying and inappropriate behaviour, he has chosen to brazen it out. He has 'no apologies for having high standards' apparently. I'll say.

The endless personal scandals that occupy journalists week on week, however, are foothills obscuring the mountainous malfeasance that is the *raison d'être* of this failed administration.

During the 2017 election campaign, I saw a voter in Barrow-in-Furness explain why he was switching his vote to the Conservatives. He had seen neighbouring Tory constituencies receiving regeneration funding and concluded that if Barrow returned a Tory MP, 'they'll look after us.' Barrow went Conservative in 2019.

Much has been written about the 'Red Wall' Conservative voters: largely patronising bunk about alienation and cultural values that had led former Labour voters to abandon their own interests in favour of tax breaks for hedge fund managers. The truth is that many of these voters were alert to the Tories' willingness to reward constituencies that voted for them at the expense of neighbouring ones that didn't. The 'levelling up' agenda that has been at the heart of the post-Brexit Conservative offer amounts to little more than vote buying and was understood as such by the voters it targeted.

This attempt to widen the Conservative base is redolent of Margaret Thatcher's sale of social housing. That too offered a direct financial reward for voting Conservative and did so at the expense of people who weren't in a position to take advantage. The difference, however, is that people actually got to buy their houses. Friday's announcement of levelling up projects reveals that the Government has pocketed the Red Wall votes and failed to come up with the goodies. As ever, the South East of England has received the lion's share of Government largesse and the North East the scraps. Any criminal knows that you have to serve

143

your clientele. A drug dealer might be wreaking havoc on an estate but his customers, at least, get their fix. Michael Gove *et al* have been doling out baggies of bicarbonate of soda to the Red Wall while the stockbroker belt parties on. As A&E departments face collapse, ministers are high on their own supply.

If areas that voted for the Tories have been stiffed, then it can be no surprise that those that didn't are treated yet more contemptuously. Twitter personality, Andrew 'Rough Trade' Davies sought this week to parlay his social media dominance into influence over UK policy by demanding that Wales receives a share of the HS2 budget. The UK Government, however, does not accept Twitter likes as legal tender and with the Tories facing electoral wipeout here, even Mr Davies' charms will not entice back the cash we have paid in.

In the face of all this, you might expect Keir Starmer to be coming on like Martin Luther, nailing a proclamation to the door of Downing Street in righteous fury at the squalid state of the nation. Instead, the Richard Briers of British politics pootled off to Davos and declared that Labour would be 'open for business'. Finding favour amongst the global elite, Starmer later opined that it was a far nicer place to be than Westminster. As the old song goes, 'He was only a toolmaker's son, but he knew how to engineer a derivatives-based financial instrument that would, in the fullness of time, provide a return to the Treasury that might allow him to look again at public sector pay demands in the future.'

Nobody benefiting from things as they are fears any accountability from the system we have. Neither electorally nor legally do we have any levers to pull that will effect substantive change in the way the resources of Britain are distributed and managed. Our politicians may not fear God anymore, we must find a way to have them fear us.

30p Lee

12 February 2023

It's fair to say that decision making in the Conservative Party is not functioning at an optimal level. Caught between terror and fury, the stricken blue whale is thrashing about as the current carries it towards its final resting place next to the Mr Whippy van on Blackpool beach.

Reaching an accommodation with mortality becomes the prime challenge for all of us as we meander towards the void, and you will have noticed that those of us with mountainous reserves of self-regard tend to struggle with it more than most.

The penny has dropped for some Tory MPs. Every couple of days one of them announces that they will be shuffling off to the great non-executive directorship in the sky before the next election. Even Nadine Dorries is, apparently, 'standing down' from whatever duties she imagines that she currently performs.

Those who remain are raging against the dying of the light with increasingly unpredictable attempts to bargain with the reaper.

As the consultant sympathetically shakes his head and ushers them towards an end-of-life counsellor, the true believers are turning, instead, to faith healers.

Over the last few years, we have seen the Boris cult, which held that Brexit could be achieved successfully if we all adopted a jolly attitude. Then came the revivalist, Liz Truss. Her prescription was to imagine that it was 1987 and ignore all economic indicators to the contrary. Sunak and Hunt are the palliative team, quietly euthanising the party on behalf of high finance whilst keeping up appearances for the relatives.

The patient's spirits must be kept up, though, and the role of Hospice Entertainer has been handed to Nottinghamshire MP and Fisher Price outrage pedlar, Lee Anderson. 30p Lee is what you are left with if you scrub the Eton sheen off Boris Johnson: a man distinguished only by his willingness to debase all around him in the pursuit of attention and validation.

Within hours of his appointment as Deputy Chair of the Conservative Party, an interview from last week had emerged in which Anderson voiced support for capital punishment. This view is espoused by many on the right and, one can assume, held privately by many more. Their reasoning is diverse: some see a deterrent effect; others insist on a morally absolute response to heinous crimes. Lee, on the other hand, supports the reintroduction of hanging on the basis that, 'Nobody has ever committed a crime after being executed.'

It is depressing to hear anybody make a statement of such banal idiocy about something as serious as taking a life, to hear it from somebody occupying a senior position in our representative democracy is shocking on a 'Frank Bough did what?' level. The motivation, though, is obvious. 'Working people', that mysterious blob of humanity to whom migrants and Meghan Markle mean more than a living wage, are assumed to be desperate for a return to capital punishment and as Lee never tires of telling us, he knows how working people think. To evidence his psychic insight into the collective consciousness of the PAYE classes, Anderson points to the fact that he has never lived more than five miles from the spot where he was born. 'What do they know of England, who only England know?' as Rudyard Kipling recently quipped on his GB News show.

If it were only England in play here, I could lob a few barbs eastwards and leave you to scour Lidl for eggs but, unfortunately, the torrent of effluent I describe above has once again been diverted our way by human sluice gate, Andrew 'ReTweet' Davies.

Despite support for capital punishment in Wales dropping below 50% for the last eight years, our own self-appointed spokesman for the workingman has been heating up his laptop lavishing praise on Anderson. Displaying sharp political instinct, Davies has drawn on the warm solidarity that Wales has always enjoyed with Conservatives from the Nottinghamshire coalfield to suggest that his new hero has captured the zeitgeist in Welsh popular opinion.

Before long, we will be enjoying the post-funereal vol-au-vents as these malevolent clowns are swept away from public office, but the tragicomic desperation that is accompanying their predictably undignified passage to oblivion must never distract from the incalculable harm their party has done over the last 13 years.

Soon, they'll see a bright light. They should shush and walk towards it, after all they won't be committing any crimes afterwards.

Quiet Pride

17 July 2022

It turns out that we are slightly inferior to the world champions. So, when we are all burned to a crisp next week and Powys is redesignated as a desert, we shall, at least, have avoided the worst-case scenario. Greta Thunberg, as it happens, was quite optimistic about Wales' prospects going into this tour.

'For Christ's sake, mun,' she urged, 'Calm down until the coaching team have had time to settle in!'

But we don't really do Scandinavian restraint here when it comes to rugby, do we? In the febrile[1] atmosphere that took hold after the loss to Italy, it seemed like we were entering the end of days. Against a backdrop of regional failure, we couldn't make sense of selections for the national team, and as they capitulated against the Italians in Cardiff, many of us feared that this time our woes were existential.

But everything is at the moment, isn't it? Even aside from the cataclysmic weather, we have an endless pandemic, governments falling, Russia threatening us with nuclear obliteration, unaffordable butter, and dachshunds everywhere.[2] As a matter of simple self-preservation, it obviously wouldn't be wise to invest your hope in the national rugby team. Far better to bask in the feel-good vibes of the football team, whose success has seemed to be in carefree contrast to the ongoing psychodrama of the WRU- that befeathered relic from a long-gone idea of our nation.

---

[1] The Welsh Government passed a law in 2016 requiring 'febrile' to be used in all rugby articles.

[2] Two years previously there were French bulldogs all over the place. Where have they gone? It's sinister.

Interest in the series in South Africa has been muted. I've had a job finding people to talk to about it and, even during the games, people's emotions haven't been on display. Yesterday, with a historic series win possible, you might have expected it to feel special but driving through the Rhondda before the game, I saw only one guy wearing a jersey, and he was sat on a wall with a face like half a tin of condemned veal. It hasn't helped that the games have been on Sky. Whether you despise the BBC for being pinko-globalists hell-bent on the destruction of our way of life, or for being Tory-enabling shills whose function is to keep the working man ignorant, it's undeniable that sporting events on the Beeb cohere us better than those on paywall channels.

So, the extraordinary journey of Wales in South Africa over the last three weeks hasn't been the water-cooler event that it deserved to be. Absolutely nobody gave our side a snowball's chance in hell of winning it. The talk after the Six Nations was of record losses and humiliation: of a side that was simply unable to compete at the top level. By kick-off for the last game, it seemed entirely plausible that Wales could win the series.

I watched the final game in Ynyshir Working Men's Club and nobody had any gripes about the outcome. The loss was taken with the humour afforded by a respectable performance. We never really looked like winning it but neither did Wales seem in danger of losing touch. As Dean next to me observed, the South Africans will be on their mettle when they are next in Cardiff. The idea that Wales are no longer competitive has been put to bed, at least for the time being.

So, what went right? Firstly, it seems that Wales have some tactical nouse now. Outmuscled upfront, the side backed themselves in the air and kicked well to create those opportunities. Second, this is now Dan Biggar's side. During the Six Nations, it seemed rather that Biggar was running around in Alun Wyn Jones' outsized boots. Now, the side is dancing to his tune. In one respect – discipline – this is a debatable plus, but in terms of commitment and belief, he has inspired Wales to overachieve. Finally, and most crucially, we have rediscovered our attacking edge. Even with possession limited by the Springbok pack, Wales looked capable of scoring tries until the dying minutes of this series.

The sky didn't fall, after all. Wales should be proud of this team and fully behind it for the campaigns ahead.[3]

---

[3] I'm apparently issuing instructions to the nation now. I can only apologise. As I say, it'd had been a rough couple of weeks.

A Poverty of Hope

19 Feb 2023

You may not, I learned this week, criticise Keir Starmer. Whilst deriding the crass machinations of the oblong-faced charlatan might seem a perfectly natural class of a thing to do, you absolutely mustn't.

Sir Keir, *not Kieth*, your name vill also go in zee book, has been anointed to deliver us from evil. The only way unto Heaven is through Him, so stop taking the piss.

As Dusty Springfield had it, the only boy who could ever teach me was the son-of-a-toolmaker. Yes he WAS!

He who speaketh against Sir Keir speaketh *for* the Tories. Now, I know some of you imagine that there are paradigms other than an exclusive, binary choice between loving Sir Keir or sacrificing your first-born child to Grant Shapps, but that is just Satan tricking you.

So, now that Jeremy Corbyn has been cast into the desert and Nicola Sturgeon is off to spend more time with her MI5 pension, let's examine the case for Sir Keir, as insisted upon by centrist dads who know what's good for us.

The first law of Keirism holds that not being Jeremy Corbyn > being anything else. Essentially, Keirites hold that if Sir Keir were to knock on the door of a hard-working, formerly Labour family in the north of England with a bag of chicken kormas and beer the conversation would go thusly,

'Eh oop, is tha the rabidly Remain Brexit spokesman for t' Labour party?'

'Hi, I'm Sir Keir. I recognise the validity of your vote on

151

Brexit and am styling the Union flag as a cape.'

'Aye, well that's as mebbe, but what about t'anti-business Trotskyite entryists in thy midst? We'll not vote for owt communist in this house!'

'May I present my credentials?'

At this, Sir Keir hands his hobnailed interlocutor a card that reads, *I am not Jeremy Corbyn.*

'Well why didn't you say, yer daft bugger? Come on in! Can I stop being Northern now?'

'Yes, you've fulfilled your role in my focus group...'

This only works thanks to the second law of Keirism, which holds that the electorate is as thick as Piers Morgan's wrists.

Here is what the *QI*-watching classes believe is going to usher in a new age of decency:

- Brexit voters now realise their mistake but are a stubborn bunch that must not be antagonised. So, in order to negotiate as near a reversal of Brexit as possible without admitting it, Sir Keir must appear at all times as if he is off to the last night of the Proms.
- It's common knowledge that Brexit-voters can be mesmerised with flags, so keep adding more and more of them, in the hope that their visual appeal will make up for the red meat racism that the Tories will be offering.
- Only offer a change of personnel. The electorate have been so thoroughly brainwashed that to suggest that their problems are caused by anything other than baddies running the show risks scaring them. Pretend that inherent decency will cure the ills of a society broken by 40 years of insane economics.
- Throw strikers under the bus. Nothing will persuade

those without union protection that their rights are being decimated, so give a nod and wink to the idea that public service workers are scroungers.

The overarching theme of this, according to the performative left, is that once in power Labour will pivot to the left and deliver a better society. The problem here, as ever, is of politicians who have mortgaged our future on an election result. What Sir Keir will find out, when in power, is that voters stupid enough to be seduced by flags will expect some racism in return for their votes. He will also discover that allowing international capital to supervise the managed decline of the UK will not result in power brokers giving us a break on the basis of his loyalty.

Starmer won the leadership of his party with 'pledges' that suggested he would pursue an agenda that would challenge the status quo. All of these have been abandoned and, this week, he told everyone who didn't like it to leave the party. Like you, I'm confused by what motivates the sort of floating voter who switches from lifetime Labour-voting to Boris Johnson, but I'm absolutely certain that pandering to such a creature is in nobody's interest.

The King of the Remainers is now, we're led to believe, an adherent of Brexit. The man named after Keir Hardie represents the workers *and* the bosses, even when the bosses are government itself. If this is where we are supposed to invest our hopes, then keep them very, very low.

A Gove Divine

When Rishi Sunak was writing prize essays at Winchester School calling for the UK to leave the European Union, he can't have imagined that he'd end up hawking sovereignty round the streets of Belfast like knock-off aftershave. His new, improved Brexit now comes with Single Market membership for Northern Ireland so the Del Boy of Downing Street is left in the unenviable position of selling Brexit with 50% less Brexit.

All the high-priced edumacating that the PM's folks invested in him seems not to have provided him with the awareness that telling 'you guys' (on this occasion the people of Northern Ireland) that they are in 'an unbelievably special position' thanks to Single Market access is not going to go unnoticed by the rest of 'us guys' who aren't.

It strikes me that Sunak isn't a solipsistic ethics-vacuum like Johnson; nor is he a froth-mouthed zealot who would sit easily in the ERG. His position, however, is entirely defined by their combined malfeasance and idiocy. Like Theresa May before him, vanity and ambition have led him to ignore the evident truth that there is no advantageous outcome to Brexit that will satisfy the people who still believe in it. Northern Ireland is where theoretical politics meets reality. Hare-brained plans might meet elevated grumbling here in Wales, perhaps peaking with a march by a few hundred people down Queen Street. Get it wrong in Belfast and bullets can start flying without notice. With that risk-assessment in place, it is telling that we have heard very little infantile squealing this week from Mark Francois, Bill Cash, Steve Baker et al. There are times, it seems, when the draping of a Union flag over a problem seems unwise even to them. With the room finally occupied by adults, the safest solution to Brexit for Northern Ireland was deemed to be as little Brexit as possible. It will be interesting to see if that idea gathers momentum elsewhere.

Johnson, of course, ran his potential objection to Sunak's protocol up the flagpole to see if it rallied support for his return to the top table. That it didn't may indicate that we are finally seeing the end of a career that would be considered a disgrace by anybody capable of feeling shame. With his behaviour during lockdown once again under scrutiny, he responded to the charge that he had misled Parliament with the typically unsubstantiated boast that he had been 'vindicated'.

For Johnson, the term 'vindicated' is indistinguishable from 'got away with it' and that he was allowed to get away with so much for so long is how history will explain a great deal of the grave problems facing us all now. It should be a matter of alarm that the opposition is proposing no constitutional reforms to facilitate the removal of bad actors from power.

Character, though, is for little people. Whilst Johnson sails off to millions on the speaking circuit, and Rees-Mogg is rewarded for lying to the queen with his own show on GB News, Michael Gove is preoccupied with the parents of truanting children. Another Brexiteer who found it convenient to keep his mouth shut about Northern Ireland this week, Gove suggests that benefits be withdrawn from the parents of children who miss school regularly. Whilst this seems straight out of the worn Tory playbook – see also teenagers becoming pregnant to secure council flats – Gove's particular take on it is revealing. To begin with, we have his blithe assertion that the parents of truants are reliant on benefits. He has crafted a solution to a problem that, by definition, only addresses it as it relates to the poor. If, though, we were to accept his proposition that truancy arises from poverty, then his solution to it is to exacerbate poverty.

So, in a crowded field, this week's exemplar of Tory

governance goes to Michael Gove. Ignoring entirely the week's significance for Brexit, of which he was a principal author, Mr Gove chose instead to propose a policy that, by its own logic, cannot work. He managed to incorporate stupidity, cruelty and self-interest into his offering and impressed the judges with his willingness to demand punctilious responsibility from the public whilst evading all accountability himself. Well done Mr Gove. Matt Hancock was ineligible for this week's prize due to imminent incarceration.[1]

---

[1] Inherent optimism is a real problem in this line of work.

Tylorstown RFC

One current truism in rugby is that the elite game is increasingly remote from the grassroots version. The contrast was certainly stark at Tylorstown RFC in Rhondda Fach where I came to watch Wales' latest capitulation to the All Blacks in the company of club stalwarts Brian Rackham and Dean Evans.

On the screen, the WRU's lavish presentation of our national game couldn't disguise the gulf in power and efficiency between the two sides. In the packed clubhouse, a stoic attitude was on display, mixed with a little consternation at Wales' shortcomings.

'We're too slow at the breakdown,' Dean noted. 'By the time we have the ball away they've set their defence.'

He wasn't wrong. At the breakdown, the All Blacks seemed not to lose an inch all afternoon. We have grown accustomed to being outmuscled in the scrummage, but today's encounter saw Wales pushed back every time the ball was taken into contact, whether attacking or in defence.

'I know we can't run every ball, but our strength is behind, not up front,' Brian opined.

In attack, Wales were running into a brick wall and with two fliers on the wings it seemed perverse that we chose to take so much possession into contact rather than turn the All Blacks with chips over their defensive line. After a protracted period of Welsh possession that seemed to seesaw endlessly between the All Blacks' 22- and 10-metre lines, Dean summed up the reality of the game.

'We've just had 17 phases of play. The All Blacks would

have scored twice with that possession.'

Although not as vulnerable as some had hoped, New Zealand did offer opportunities to Wales throughout the game and to be fair to the home side, Wales showed alertness when these arose, with Tomos Williams and newcomer Rio Dyer particularly lively. The problem was that in the meat and potatoes struggle for overall momentum, Wales seemed to be playing uphill all afternoon.

Each Welsh score was countered immediately by a New Zealand side that only had to enter the Welsh 22 to be assured of points.

'They play at high intensity all the time,' as Dean had it.

The final 20 minutes saw New Zealand stretch away in a fashion all too familiar to the Welsh faithful.

'Turn it off!' came the cry from one despairing wag, and while the 23:55 scoreline was harsh on a Welsh side that had shown flashes of enterprise, it fairly reflected the visitors' superiority.

But Welsh rugby is about more than televised humiliations in Cardiff. Here at Tylorstown RFC, they welcomed 2000 people to their bonfire on Friday night and the club, in partnership with local organisations, offers courses ranging from food preparation to First Aid and Welsh. The club, as Dean explains, sees itself as the hub of a local community that has been overlooked for regeneration time and again.

'We'll be offering warm bank facilities when the weather turns.'

A year ago, the club took the initiative to start a mini rugby section and, in a valley short of facilities for youngsters, 200 children have flocked to be part of the game. Dean is particularly proud that 50 of these comprise a thriving girls' section.

The wreckage of international hopes that I seem to describe

every time we play recently can be a depressing affair, and fears for the future of the grassroots game are echoed in every club I visit. Here in Tylorstown, though, I found cause for optimism that transcended the woes of Wayne Pivac's team. Children in Wales still want to play this game, and adults still want to teach them how. As the plastic glasses were being swept up in the stadium 20 miles to the south, a singer was coming on in the back room of Tylorstown RFC, where rugby remains at the centre of a way of life.

Stop the Boats

12 March 2023

When Donny worries that they are being attacked by Nazis in *The Big Lebowski,* John Goodman's Walter reassures him that they are only nihilists.

'I mean, say what you want about the tenets of National Socialism, Dude, at least it's an ethos…'

Wading through Suella Braverman's latest torrent of effluent this week, I reminded myself of that exchange as a means of maintaining sufficient equilibrium to carry on with my day.

The *Big Lebowski* nihilists were performance artists and that is the sensible way to interpret the government's proposals on immigration. Braverman, Sunak and the rest of the clown car occupants know right well that nothing announced this week can be enacted, as it will be slapped down by the courts.

The sole purpose of this grubby enterprise is to pressgang us all into a performance for a dwindling reserve of voters whose bigotry can be activated to propel them to a voting booth. Everybody has been assigned a role in this pantomime, and the cast list is as follows:

Braverman: Maverick defender of the shores; Bargain basement Boudica – says the unsayable; nuance-resistant owner of one broad brush.

Starmer: Lefty lawyer; Baron of the Blob – personifies tedious objections to fantastical notions whilst simultaneously lending them credibility by engaging.

Lineker: Totemic Wokelord; Prince Harry stand-in – responds metronomically to any provocation; sofa-bound avatar of an imaginary elite.

You & Me: The chorus; Aristophanes' frogs – tweet outrage furiously; fret we are descending to the political tone of the Weimar Republic.

Small-Boatgoing Migrants: scenery.

The key to consuming this low-rent production lies in recognising its paltry ambition. Its authors are cognisant, not only that the policies are a sham, but that their purpose is not even to win an election but, rather, to save the seats of a large enough rump of Tory MPs that the party remains viable.

If this happy conclusion strikes you as too optimistic, then I point you towards the behaviour of those Tories who have carved out a public profile. Nadine Dorries is now a televangelist for Boris Johnson on Talk TV, whilst GB News has signed Jacob Rees-Mogg, Esther McVey, and Philip Davies. Even 30p Lee has secured himself a contract to present a show called *The Real World with Lee Anderson*, presumably a travel documentary in which he visits it for the first time. Expect Andrew RT Davies' Twitter feed to go into overdrive as he pitches 'Yesterday's Wales Tomorrow' for the coveted 4 a.m. slot up against *Farming Today*.

18 months out from the election, a further 25 Tory MPs have declared that they won't be standing, including Dehenna Davison who, at 29, was once seen as representing the party's future. The jig is most assuredly up, and anything you hear coming from the party at this point needs to be contextualised within the prospect of its upcoming electoral annihilation.

This is not to say you shouldn't be sickened by the depths to which these people will sink, but we do have the choice not to participate in their artificial controversies. The slogan for this week's effort is 'Stop the Boats'. By the time of the election, you will feel as if that phrase has been tattooed on the inside of your eyelids as it is wheeled out relentlessly and presented with overtly fascistic aesthetics to stir up the sort of outrage that might, just might, penetrate the vague fog of racist Uncle Graham's dotage and propel him on a somnambulant wander to the polling station.

Crass as the slogan is, you needn't even worry that it marks some new, cutting edge, possibly effective, direction in populist politics. The precise phrase 'Stop the Boats' was used by Australian PM Tony Abbott to win power in 2013. So, this Tory gambit is a cover version. Even if Lynton Crosby isn't behind its resurrection, the party clearly hasn't evolved beyond his influence and part of why this week's presentation jarred is because of how dated it seemed.

There's going to be more of this. As the polls engender terror in unemployable Tory MPs, pressure will grow to mount an ever more desperate rearguard action. By polling day you'd be forgiven for fearing that a flotilla of Albanians are off the coast of Kent intent on invading the nation's remaining libraries to revise Roald Dahl books.[1] It will be all heat and no light.

Keep cool, though. Poor Donny died of fright because he thought the Nazis were after him. When you feel your blood pressure rising remember...

They're just nihilists.

---

[1] 'Woke' new editions of Dahl classics were the week's other media obsession. The reissue of the originals a few weeks later by the same publisher revealed that this controversy, like almost everything we read, was a PR stunt.

Birth, School, Work, Death

19 March 2023

Like you, I will always have a special place in my heart for Jeremy Hunt. With the news full of striking workers and collapsing public services, it's easy to forget the worry that can be caused by capping a person's annual pension contribution at £40k per year. Here in the Rhondda, this week's budget was met with such unbounded joy that an expectant mother gave birth on the shop floor of the Morrisons Daily in Pontygwaith, promptly naming the baby Jeremy.

Baby Jeremy himself was dismayed to learn that he should have been aiming for a gestation period of two years in order to take advantage of the Chancellor's enhanced childcare offer but resolved to enter the 'Great British Workforce' in the meantime, provided he doesn't succumb to rickets.

The Chancellor seemed to be under the impression that his budget represented the dawning of a brighter future for us all. Adopting his best approximation of an upbeat tone, the ascetic Mr Hunt delivered his nondescript package of half-measures and deferred solutions as if they were a reward for the financial chaos we have all been suffering since his predecessor discovered that the bond market didn't share his penchant for fiscal edgelordery.

As with last week's fantastical ordure concerning refugees, there was a distinct suspicion that very little being proposed was actually going to happen. The extension of childcare to younger children was the flagship policy for the masses and was safely punted beyond the date of the next election.

Hunt was keen to herald the 'help' he will be offering to the disabled so that they can find work. The specifics of this, however, were alarmingly vague. The Work Capability Assessment is to be scrapped but with no indication as to what system will replace it. Alongside this, benefits claimants can look forward to a 'strengthened' sanctions regime which will, increasingly, be automated.

'Conservatives believe,' the Chancellor reminded us, 'that work is a virtue.'

Well, not according to my Bible, but with charity, hope, prudence, temperance, fortitude, and justice plainly off the table, Mr Hunt could perhaps rely on faith to explain how abolishing a test of fitness to work is going to make anyone fitter for work.

The rationale offered on Tuesday was that new modes of working, such as Teams and Zoom, will liberate employment-hungry disabled people from dependence on the state. Presumably, these potential workers have failed to notice such technological developments themselves so they can count themselves lucky that the new sanction-issuing AI programme is there to help them out. After all, if anything is crying out to be stripped of its humanity it's the DWP, hitherto the governmental branch of the Samaritans.

Brexit got a mention, not of course as the reason for our labour shortage, heaven forfend, but because the Chancellor has found a way to reduce the taxation on draught beer that would have been forbidden by the EU. Here it is at last, the Brexit benefit. I hope that Plaid Cymru have taken note of this as it is plainly the key to unshackling a nation from its supranational oppressor. No financial planning at all will be necessary to emerge victorious from an independence campaign. Adam Price need only to hold aloft two pints of beer, one 11 pence cheaper than the other, and the case will be won.

Still, I suppose Hunt didn't crash the pound and on recent form we can take that as some sort of win. Keir Starmer's response, however, was magisterial. Rising to the despatch box draped in a red flag and flanked by a politburo of zealots who pledge to bring the old order to its knees, Starmer unveiled plans to organise the southeast of England into a collective farm where the landlord class will be forcibly re-educated and brought to enlightenment by the masses. Promising to redistribute wealth from executed bankers to all corners of the realm, Starmer was interrupted by an ecstatic Stephen Kinnock who screamed,

'Caws a bara!' repeatedly and was joined in his call by a parliamentary Labour Party that stands ready to liberate the British worker by any means necessary. They'll raise the minimum wage to a tenner an hour, apparently.

Vive Le Mob

26 March 2023

Poor King Charles, having been wrenched away from Wales to take over the failing family concern he inherited from his mom, he's not allowed to go on his holidays to France lest he fall victim to a *Les-Misérables*-themed flash mob. A cynical observer might suspect that Emmanuel Macron's real concern wasn't Charles and Camilla being hauled off to the guillotine by yellow-vested sans-culottes, but the PR implications of having to entertain royalty at the Palace of Versailles. It's an awkward look for the leader of a revolutionary republic at the best of times, but when you are already coming across like the bastard offspring of Princess Margaret and Justin Bieber you don't want to be photographed with a sparkly-hatted personification of divine patronage. *Non.*

The French people, you see, will be watching, and the optics work both ways. As much as Macron cannot avoid the gaze of the citizenry, neither can he avert his eyes from them. The people are *there*, in public spaces putting the fear of God into anyone trying to diminish their prospects of happiness. The simple visibility of the French public in political life serves them well. In the UK, where many have been persuaded that acts of protest are not only futile but impolite and embarrassing, our politicians can avoid us altogether for five years at a time. By conducting politics through the media and online, dissent has been decanted into sealed echo chambers that rage away while the business of state is conducted without interference.

Life is much easier for politicians if they are permitted to fabricate a fictional version of the people they are supposed to serve. In Mao's China, people were urged to 'learn from the example of Comrade Lei Feng', an ordinary soldier whose every act was unselfish and whose devotion to Mao was unparalleled. For years he was promoted by the government as a role model and is celebrated to this day in some regions of China. There is no evidence that Lei Feng ever existed, and the diary published after his supposed death in 1962 is widely accepted as a state forgery.

In the UK, we are encouraged to believe that the likes of 30p Lee Anderson represent a vast hinterland of xenophobic, reactionary peasants whose instincts form the bedrock of 'British' character and are served by the ruling party. But Anderson hasn't been carried aloft by a crowd of people who want their voices to be heard, he's been installed by an almost comically privileged elite to persuade the electorate that their worst, most self-defeating notions are what define them.

Meanwhile, the business of Westminster grinds on without interfacing with living, breathing commoners at all. This week, Alexander Boris de Pfeffel Johnson was 'grilled' by the Parliamentary Privileges Committee with plaudits going to Harriet Harman, who is the niece of the Earl of Longford, for her dogged questioning.

During the hearing, the division bell sounded, and participants filed into the chamber to wave through the reversal of four years' government policy on Brexit before returning to hear Johnson's evident irritation at the impertinence of it all.

With the broadcast media focused on the hearings, Rishi Sunak took the opportunity to release his tax details, showing earnings of £4.8 million over the last three years, on which he was taxed at 22% thanks to the higher-rate tax cut he voted for in 2016.

You might wonder what the effect of a few hundred thousand of us regularly turning up outside Parliament might have on its occupants. Would they feel the weight of their responsibility if they had to confront the citizenry in numbers? If they could see us out of the leaded windows of committee rooms, and hear the rumble of our discontent as they stepped on to the Commons

Terrace to enjoy the wine we paid for, would their sinews stiffen in fear of wronging us?

Not so long ago, Prince Charles was going to be King George, fearing that his first name was too linked with the revolutionary decapitation of Charles 1. That he chose to persist with it suggests that royal Charlies have benefited from a recent cultural emphasis on tradition and stability at the expense of social history and societal progress.

We are looking forward to retiring five years later than the French and on around five grand a year less in state pension. Plus ça change…

Out of the Gloom

13 Nov 2022

Ynyshir & District Workingmen's Club likes to watch games with the house lights off, cinema style, so there was an eerie atmosphere as the bugler sounded the Last Post before today's clash with Argentina. The subsequent silence was observed flawlessly, save for a quiet and, I suspect, involuntary, 'Go on, boy!' when the camera paused on Louis Rees-Zammit.

With Argentina buoyant after victory over England last week, hopes were as subdued as the lighting. Darren felt that the visitors would have the psychological edge.

'They've had big victories recently. Argentina have always been physically strong but now they have mental strength too.'

We didn't go into how last week's mauling from the All Blacks might have affected Wales' collective mentality, but it certainly didn't do much for mine.

Rugby will always throw up surprises, that's the thrill of it, but Wayne Pivac's Welsh sides don't seem to follow any sort of narrative thread at all. Players pop up in positions where they've never played, star performers are dropped for reasons nobody understands, and the lethargy of one week's performance can give way to renewed intensity a week later.

This time, Alun Wyn Jones had been dismissed from the match day squad, Rees-Zammit was asked to try his luck at full back, and Dillon Lewis replaced Tomas Francis at tight head.

This last change seemed fully vindicated when Wales dismantled Argentina at the first scrum. Set piece failure has been endemic in recent years, so this came as a welcome surprise, albeit one spoiled by a shambolic effort at the subsequent lineout.

Rees-Zammit's frustration is sometimes visible when he's stood by the touchline wondering if the ball will ever come his way, so it was no surprise to see him taking advantage of the latitude that a full back can enjoy to make an early, scything incursion through the Argentinian defence. With his own defensive game improving all the time, it makes sense to ensure that such a threatening attacker is not dependent on the run of play for his opportunities. At full back, he can seek them out.

After repeated penalties for offside had gifted Argentina a six-point lead, a prolonged Welsh attack recalled last week's failure to penetrate the last line of defence. Wales seemed composed, however, and had the confidence to spurn opportunities to kick points in the hope that their sustained pressure would pay off, and pay off it did with Taulupe Faletau going over from a lineout to celebrate his birthday with a try.

With a 10-6 lead at half-time the club was warming up. While the back room was boisterous as a younger crowd enjoyed Newcastle beating Chelsea, the rugby devotees, who included Ponty, Llanelli and Wales legend Gary 'Boomer' Jones, were allowing cautious hope to be entertained.

'10-6! We'll take that!' Darren announced, bringing back a pint of Madri to go with the one he'd forgotten he'd bought before his expedition to the Gents.

Outside, vapers and smokers commented on the menacingly warm weather, and a miscreant was informed that the licence only allowed for drinks to be brought outside between March 1st and October 31st. I scanned Aberrhondda Road for the Feds but he got away with it…this time.

I experience real fear at the outset of the second half whenever Wales play; so often it seems that we emerge from the break and ship points, regardless of how well the first half might have gone. This time, however, it was the unfortunate Juan Cruz

Mallía whose fluffed clearance gave Tomos Williams a charge down score so simple he seemed almost embarrassed as he walked back.

There was still jeopardy in the game, as Argentina closed the gap to seven points through a converted Chaparro try, but Wales had remembered how to defend and, with Priestland on to direct their play, managed to close out the win professionally.

Given Australia's loss to Italy, Wales must be hoping that today's resurgence has laid the groundwork to rescue their autumn campaign. Whether by accident or design, the changes made this week might be the way forward.

Antisocial Media

3 July 2022

If you ever look at the state of the UK and wonder how we've got here, have a read through your local Facebook page and reflect on the terrifying reality that all those people have a vote. Social media has lifted the lid on the inner lives of our neighbours and their thought processes are now on display for all to see, preserved forever on Mark Zuckerberg's servers. Our wildest, least considered utterances are indelibly etched into immortality, beyond the reach of any deletion tool.

Tracing the family tree will be a very different experience for our descendants. The most troubling aspect of it for most of us is deciphering the copperplate handwriting in the 1891 census.

'So, Great-Uncle Ezekiel was a sniper, cool! Oh, hang on, it says pauper…'

Give it a few years and genealogy websites will be flogging off timelines of the deceased to unsuspecting family historians so they can search for shared characteristics with their ancestors and feel some connection to the grand sweep of human experience.

'Okay honey, I know it was expensive, but I've paid for Aunt Courtney's 2023 socials. It was such a pivotal time in history, I feel like the kids should know how our family fitted in to it all.'

'I absolutely get that darling; I don't mind missing out on our holiday this year. That was when World War 3 started and the old United Kingdom began to break up. Can I look with you?'

1st January 2023

CourtneyRocks: Happy New Year to everyone in Llareggub Community Group, except the snakes. You know who you are. 00:00

CourtneyRocks: Can whoever has parked their car outside the food distribution point please move it as the army will need to get in with our delivery in the morning. A little consideration? 00:05

CourtneyRocks: Just a reminder that the recent thermonuclear attack is no excuse not to clean up after your dog. YOU KNOW WHO YOU ARE. Fuming. 06:01

ConcernedMum: Couldn't agree more with CourtneyRocks about disgusting individuals who don't clean up after their dogs. Llareggub used to be such a lovely place to bring up kids. 06:02

CourtneyRocks: Just a little message to those sad people who accused me of running an alt. account on here. Look after your own business, I'm just a busy mum who is concerned about Llareggub. 08:17

CourtneyRocks: RIP the population of Greater Manchester 🙁 10:28

ConcernedMum: OMG, I loved Coronation Street! 10.29

CourtneyRocks: ANOTHER pile of dog mess on the Graig. WHAT ABOUT THE CHILDREN?!!!!! Seriously thinking of naming and shaming. 10:45

And if dissociation from world events isn't concerning enough, it's nothing to the online behaviour of people who *are* engaged with the wider picture. Political discussion groups on Facebook routinely describe themselves as forums for civil debate, often with lofty aspirations about their role in participatory democracy. Newcomers to them tend to make the mistake of taking this at face value.

> **Newcomer1981:** Hi everyone, thanks for letting me join the group, I'm looking forward to contributing! What do we all think about the prospects of a progressive alliance? Is that something the Conservatives should be concerned about?
>
> **EnochWasRight:** Ha ha ha! Another one!
>
> **Newcomer1981:** Sorry, another what?
>
> **EnochWasRight:** Treehugging snowflake. I suppose we're all supposed to be worried about your pronouns?
>
> **Lenin1917:** I see Enoch has woken up in the care home. Brought round your copy of the Daily Heil, have they?
>
> **EnochWasRight:** Oh dear, once again The Left have no argument so are resorting to insults. How sad.
>
> **Scotsgirl:** Perhaps we could just engage with the question?
>
> **Superyoon:** Oh, Wee Jimmie Krankie wants to 'engage with the question'.
>
> **Scotsgirl:** Eh?
>
> **Superyoon:** You're obviously angling for a referendum.

Etc. etc. etc.[1]

When Carol Hanisch asserted that 'the personal is political' in 1970, she hadn't been privy to just how personally unpleasant many of us can be when offered a platform for our views. So, why have we become so toxic?

Socialists will point to the degrading effects on society of an exploitative economic system; conservatives will zone in on a lack of personal responsibility, while nationalists will find blame on the other side of the nearest border.

All of us, though, for the first time in human history, will leave everything we have said to be discovered after we are gone. I don't know about you, but I'm more than a little uneasy at what they will find.

---

[1] I spent half of 2021 in Facebook jail for rising to the bait in political groups. In Merthyr Tydfil one morning I recognised another sane member of a particularly vitriolic group called UK Politics. I greeted her in warm solidarity before appreciating that recognising somebody from their profile pic is not the same thing as actually knowing them. She looked terrified. Mind you, I have form for this. On my 30th birthday in the Hyatt hotel in Birmingham, several bottles of red in, I cheerfully greeted a bloke in a large hat I recognised from somewhere I couldn't quite place. It was Boy George.

Zero Sum Game

2 April 2023

Remember when facing 34 criminal charges for claiming a tax deduction on money you gave your lawyer to pay off the porn star you had a fling with might adversely affect your prospects of elected public office?

For anybody born this century, that scenario must be as alien as dial phones and a regulated rental sector. America's latest deep dive into Donald J. Trump's personal life is only the latest political scandal to leave us all feeling as if we have fallen into a stagnant pond every time we switch on the news. But the relentless vileness of politicians the world over is nothing new. The greasy-pole scaling shysters have beset us since Classical times and were probably even worse when there was nobody to write it down. Winning popularity contests on the basis that you know better than everyone else isn't a proper job and we should expect no more in terms of morality from them than we do, say, stand-up comedians.

What's changed is that we are now content to expect less. Political commentators in America expect the sight of Trump's tiny hands poking through a pair of handcuffs to be an electoral asset to him in the upcoming Presidential race. For his supporters, the entire legal establishment is corrupt so any charges against their champion can be dismissed as politically motivated and without merit. Trump, of course, long ago noted that he could shoot someone on Fifth Avenue and his numbers would go up, so the wider question in play here is whether the Donald's political instincts remain disturbingly on point.

During Boris Johnson's recent Partygate hearings I noticed that his supporters weren't interested in whether he was guilty or not. Their loyalty was inspired by admiration of a man whom they believed to be exempt from the paltry rules to which the rest of us are subject by dint of his inherent greatness. Johnson himself gave the impression that it was unreasonable for anybody to expect him to be consistent because, after all, he was *Boris Johnson.*

For all Johnson's misdeeds, however, he hasn't yet attempted to incite an armed coup, so the stateside example of an irrational electorate is playing out for rather higher stakes.

Politics is heading towards a zero-sum game whereby the outcomes are: you win, or you go to jail. Trump's 'lock her up' rally chants at Hillary Clinton may seem ironic in the current context but, in truth, he read the runes of public sentiment. For most of us now, political disagreement is couched in terms of criminality and our opponents have become beyond the pale.

This leaves us all in a situation so tribal that policies and matters of character become meaningless. Trump's economic position has veered sharply to the left as he seeks to outmanoeuvre Republican rivals who threaten public health programmes that many older voters depend upon. Johnson's original 'levelling-up' plans would have cost a fortune, but he saw them as the price of keeping hold of the northern English contingent of his tribe.

The UK, of course, hasn't been levelled up and neither did Trump reindustrialise the USA. So, what inspires the blind devotion that sees him on course to be the Republican candidate again? The answer, I think, lies in a generalised powerlessness that seems to characterise the 21st Century experience for many of us. The last 25 years have seen societal changes that have been bewilderingly rapid. Very few of these, however, have come about through the political process. Tech companies and financial institutions hold power over our lives that cannot be effectively countered by any democratic means that we currently possess – ask Liz Truss who was defenestrated by the bonds market within weeks. Our own prospects for employment, housing, and even dating, are increasingly dependent on algorithms that we don't understand, and with which we cannot bargain.

So, the concept of a maverick is appealing; someone who has personal agency in a society that seems increasingly to deny it. When the Trumps and Johnsons of the world do bad things, many are less impressed by their moral failings than by their seeming success in getting away with them.

Wales v Georgia

20 November 2022

There must have been a time, once, when following international rugby in Wales was done for pleasure. I don't know about you, but trying to scrape a living in an economic hellscape during the dank gloom of November is about enough for me, without my scant leisure time being overwhelmed by national failure on a hitherto unimaginable scale.

I've been here for the cricket score losses to southern hemisphere sides, the Samoan embarrassments, Fiji at the World Cup, and even Italy last year. All of that seemed explicable in terms of the games themselves. Selection issues could be debated, another coach could be sacrificed, and we'd regain respectability in a game that we loved regardless of fortune. This feels different.

Some months ago, there was a lot of talk about separating governance of the elite game from that of the grassroots clubs. The inference was that the parochial amateurism of the clubs was stifling the professional game, upon which they depend for their funding. My remit in these articles is to watch international games at clubs and pubs to give a flavour of how supporters are feeling about them. Well, I can report that they are feeling nothing.

Today, I was at Llanidloes RFC in Powys. I've been here before, and it's reliably packed for international games. In an area not renowned for its rugby, international day has always drawn people who are motivated by cultural attachment as much as they are by the game itself. Watching the team is an opportunity to express love for Wales and it's been embraced here by locals and incomers alike.

I watched the game with the club treasurer, Peadar: a rugby fanatic who hails from Northern Ireland but wears red if he isn't

179

in green. Glancing around the sparsely attended clubhouse, Peadar explained the impact that today's meagre bar takings would have on Llanidloes RFC. Energy bills are about to increase, and the club has ambitious plans for its youth section, so Peadar has a job on allocating funds to keep everything running as it should.

I can almost hear you.

'It's only Georgia, of course there were less people in...'

I want to believe that too, but the picture I'm seeing during this is of a nation disinterested in how Wales perform. From Tylorstown to Llanidloes, I see clubs that are successfully acting as hubs of their local communities and providing social cohesion during a time of upheaval and uncertainty. Increasingly, though, they are doing this without any reference to the professional game which seems to be operating in a realm of remote dysfunction.

With the regional game routinely played in empty stadia and away games requiring a flight, often to Africa, it's not unreasonable to question what service the professional game in Wales is actually offering to its customers. A corporate, professional offering at regional level was supposed to be the price of a national side that would inspire the grassroots game. From my perspective, it seems that the organisation of community clubs puts the professional game to shame. Whilst the clubs can attract youngsters through their doors in droves and offer services to their communities that are genuinely transformational, the regions seem to chunter along in a netherworld of meaningless excuses for commercial and sporting failure. It was painful to contrast the passion and joy of the Georgian setup with the hollow media-speak of the Welsh management after the game.

I should be telling you how the punters in Llanidloes were shocked and dismayed by today's performance. As a writer[1] and a

---

[1] Oooh, get you!

fan, I want to relate the passionate debates I heard about where Wales went wrong. I can't do that because none of it happened. Everyone was keen to talk about their club because their club means the world to them. What was transpiring on the big screen seemed to be from another universe.

Shaky & Carol: The New Resistance

9 April 2023

On the 10th anniversary of Margaret Thatcher's death, the time seems ripe for a reassessment of the 1980s and how they shaped the world we live in now. What times they were, as the post-war consensus was torn apart by a socially awkward woman with daddy issues, they threw up compelling images that signified our passing from one age to another.

From the death of working-class culture at Orgreave, to the coked-up bonanza on the trading floor of the City, we have been served up a narrative that has Thatcher in the vanguard of inevitable change. Cooperative endeavour was a pipe dream, we are told, that ran contrary to the individualistic fundamentals of human nature. If you were fool enough to spend your nights in a working man's club with a meat pie and a pint when you could have been off to Club Tropicana in a DeLorean then you didn't deserve a pair of red braces.

History, though, is written by the winners and it won't tell you that at least 50% of Wham! was in the Young Communist League or that meat pies now cost £8000.[1]

George Michael's revolutionary tendencies are proving not to be unique amongst the pantheon of 1980s mainstream entertainment. Who would have guessed that when *Countdown* contestants received a 'D' from Prestatyn's Carol Vorderman, she was muttering 'dialectical materialism' under her breath? Here she is this week putting her 750,000 Twitter followers straight about Tory claims on water quality:

---

[1] A Lancashire pub had announced the availability of an £8k pie topped with gold leaf.

@carolvorders

Tory LIES via @DefraGovUK

"We've made HUGE progress on water quality."
@theresecoffey says

FACTS:
Number of rivers reaching 'Good' ecological quality.

2012 = 24%
2014 = 19%
2019 = 14%
2027 = 6% (current government projection)

Data courtesy **@Feargal_Sharkey**

You'll note that to find accurate data on the subject she had to consult the lead singer of The Undertones, whose perfect cousin was unavailable for comment having been exposed for passing off fur-lined sheepskin jackets as PPE under a contract awarded by Matt Hancock.

Ponder how the course of history might have been changed had the entertainment wing of 1980s socialism not been left to Ben Elton (an embarrassment to Bens everywhere) and Paul Weller. If Michael Foot had cottoned on that the sweetheart of teatime TV could be mobilised to agitate the bovine masses to stand up for their birthright, we may never have had to endure a single episode of *The Apprentice.*

This week we learned that what they were actually doing behind the green door was conspiring to bring down banking cartels that extract labour from the proletariat without regard for the communal cost. Cardiff's Shakin' Stevens has released an uncompromising work of anti-capitalist agitprop[2] that has drawn approval from the Sleaford Mods and Ian McNabb.

If the double-denimed king of Christmas discos is taking up the cudgels of revolt, we must heed his call. I mean, what more do you need?

We observe the rampant corruption and incompetence in Westminster as if through a telescope, trying to work out how much of it is going to affect life here in Wales and baffled as to how people like that end up in positions of responsibility. We look around us at struggling public services and failed local businesses, but are told by the London media that what we really care about is small boats, or whether Harry and Meghan attend the Coronation.

The wave of change that started in the 1980s is finally breaking over the polluted beaches of the UK and there's precious little left to defend any of us from its consequences. Wales never bought into the rhetoric of Thatcherism so it's perfectly natural for our mainstream celebrities to be saying what sounds like plain, common sense to most of us. Remember, however, what Gary Lineker has just gone through. The merest peep of dissent from well-known figures in England brings down the attack dogs of the *Daily Mail* to try to shut them up, along with the platforms that employ them.

Shaky and Carol are figures from the cultural centre of British life as it existed just a few years ago. They now stand as outsiders in a UK that has no centre and a rapidly diversifying culture. When the reckoning comes, they're definitely ours.

---

[2] 2023 single 'It All Comes Round'.

All That Glitters

16 April 2023

The opposite of love is indifference, and it would seem that King Charles is feeling its sharpened tooth as a poll suggests only nine per cent of Britons are excited at the prospect of his Coronation.

Here in Wales, where the monarchical footnote has been serving the world's longest apprenticeship, only four Coronation events have been registered and, I don't know about you, but I'm yet to hear anyone mention it at all.

Charles was conceived around the time that India gained its independence, so when his mother ascended to the throne in 1953 there was already a feeling that the jig was up for the international reach of Imperial pomp. It was slow dying, however, and people could be relied upon to fork out for bunting and Union flag place mats at the Silver Jubilee and Charles' first wedding. Queen Victoria's idea that the royals should serve as a model for the nation's family life still had some currency in 1981.

Pageantry, we were told, gave the UK a unique place in the world. Originally, the idea was to show off all the stuff that had been nicked from around the globe as a reminder of who ran the show. While the empire disappeared the spectacle carried on, at vast expense, as we were assured that it was the prime driver of tourism to the nation. So, within Charles' lifetime, the ceremonial doings of his family have devolved from imperial statecraft on the level of a US presidential inauguration, to occasional competition for the Porthcawl Elvis Festival.

It is, therefore, extremely inconvenient that a prominent tourist from Scranton, Pennsylvania seems to have gone to some lengths to give Charles' celebrations a swerve. The breathless

185

outrage of GBeebies grifters at President Biden's no-show is predictably baseless in historical precedent. US presidents do not routinely attend British coronations. The optics of Biden's jolly in Ireland, however, do seem to suggest a less than reverent attitude towards the sceptred isle.

For a start-off, Biden's reason for not attending the Coronation is that he couldn't face the trip so soon after his visit to Ireland. I mean, where are his priorities? If you are offered free tickets to the Porthcawl Elvis Festival, you don't go on a pub-crawl in Bridgend the week before and duck out of it.

If Biden hadn't done enough to leave the right-wing press with suspicious minds, his latest flame turned out to be Gerry Adams.

Again, there's nothing new about American presidents Irishing around in the run-up to elections. The Irish-American electorate expects it. What's different, though, is that Biden explicitly emphasises his Irish roots and downplays his English ancestry.

This reluctance to identify with England, and by extension Britain, is indicative that the British brand has ceased to be merely tarnished in the international court of opinion and is now toxic.

Anyone who travels will be painfully aware of the pitying giggles that a UK passport elicits around large parts of the world and it's increasingly worth the time to explain where and what Wales is if someone asks where you are from. An Irish passport, a few words of Welsh, or Scots can be a get-out-of-jail-free card from being identified with the anachronistic attitudes of Boris Johnson and Nigel Farage.

The Koh-i-Noor diamond will apparently be absent from Queen Mary's crown when Camilla becomes queen, and inherent to that decision is the acknowledgement that the proceedings represent something taboo and publicly unacceptable on the world stage. For, if the Elizabethan age had a purpose, then it was surely to sever Britain's future from its imperial past and demonstrate to the world that the country had learned from its misdeeds. Instead, national institutions have clung stubbornly to the accoutrements of empire.

Eddie Izzard once noted that when the world was enthralled by the genius of working-class, British creatives in the 1960s, the Establishment missed a trick. If the queen had hopped in an E-Type and learned to clap on the offbeat, then the privileged end of society might have been jolted from its torpor and pointed towards a future grounded in reality. Instead, they doubled down as the world moved past them and are now defended by a shrinking band of elderly obsessives and 'royal experts' whose livelihoods depend upon justifying absurdity.

King Charles ordered research into royal links to slavery last week. The world at large, however, made its minds up about the moral qualities of British imperialism long ago.

When the king dons his coronational jumpsuit and fulfils what he imagines to be his destiny, it will be to disinterest at home and mounting derision abroad. Not only has the royal ship sailed, it has sunk, with international goodwill to the UK onboard.

Postcard from Lipsi

14 May 2023

I'm sensitive that you must become resentful of my weekly missives from the enviable perch of Rhondda Fach, playground of the carefree, so this week's piece comes to you from Lipsi, an island in the Aegean Sea where you can't get a slice of corned beef pie for love nor money.

Tramping barely paved roads between one paradisiacal cove and another, nodding at sage-looking goats, and dodging sun-peeled vehicles that wouldn't pass an MOT in the Valleys even if you were on the council, there remain plenty of features that seem oddly familiar.

For a start, how were there ever enough people here to justify the ludicrous number of churches that dot the hillsides, aside from the gigantic one that dominates the only village?

When my mother was on childhood visits 'back home' from Birmingham in the 1950s, she soon learned to hide out at Auntie May's on a Sunday. Mamgu's observance of the Sabbath ran to five visits to Ebenezer Chapel down the hill in Tylorstown, and a ban on activities like knitting for the entire household.

Her devotion was a product of the last Revival, in 1905, and despite many demolitions, the sheer volume of chapel buildings in Wales always has me wondering about the fervour that gripped the nation during its successive waves of spiritual awakening. Religion has fallen so far from favour in Western society that it's impossible to imagine the sheer energy that drove the construction and use of all these buildings not so long ago. We are told that courtrooms closed down for lack of criminal cases, and pubs emptied as Wales looked to the heavens for salvation from the depredations of industrial exploitation.

There are Greek flags fluttering from many of the hillside churches in Lipsi; sending a clear message that the civic culture of the place is founded on its spiritual character. The boat that brings you here hugs the Turkish coast and over there flies the star and crescent of the Ottoman Empire that ran this vulnerable little place for 400 years until they were supplanted by the Catholic Italians. Only in 1948 did the fiercely Orthodox island become part of Greece itself.

The Wi-Fi I'm sending this over is an EU provision that ensures far-flung areas of the community have access to digital infrastructure. There's a fragility to places like this that illuminates the purpose of the EU in a way that the UK always seemed to obscure. There are no European flags here, just occasional acknowledgements that helpful initiatives came by way of Brussels.

Power and allegiance shift around us over time. You can, I've found, provoke fury by calling Tylorstown Tip 'Old Smokey'. Nuance of style and preference, however, are a different matter from coercion. Telling the difference is an exercise of emotion. On my EU-funded internet, I'm reading of a legal challenge to the promotion of Bannau Brycheiniog as the name of our national park near Brecon, and my spidey senses don't have to be at their peak to discern bullying when I see it. There is no scenario whereby the foregrounding of *Cymraeg* is the remotest threat to either the English language, or to financial interests in the nation. To my shame I don't have the language, but the more of it I see, the more I acquire and the richer I become.

Our chapels may lie largely empty nowadays, but the nonconformist instinct that birthed them is an inheritance we can draw on if we choose. Greece, you might remember, was supposed to be the most oppressed of all EU nations – the term 'Brexit' was a variation on 'Grexit' from the referenda that

189

decided Greece's continued membership. I don't see enforced language or flags here though, any more than I saw them anywhere in the UK before we exited the union. In Wales, on the other hand, I see an insecure, overbearing UK Establishment going into conniptions if we so much as change the name of a leisure destination.

Now, if you'll excuse me, I have to continue my negotiations with the nymph Calypso, who is threatening my detention here for seven years.

Lowering the Tone

22 November 2022

Approaching Cardiff's Four Elms pub in the gathering gloom, it was difficult to know what to expect from Wales yesterday. If they had been unremittingly awful all year then we'd be emotionally inured against the sort of horror show that unfolded in the second half, but they haven't, have they? It's only a few months since Wayne Pivac's side was over in South Africa, burying the memory of their Six Nations loss to Italy under a pile of plaudits. They can be tenacious and efficient, as we saw against Argentina a couple of weeks ago.

As we arrived at the pub, the landlord emerged to look around outside.

'Match day and it's dead; a ghost town!' he complained.

Inside, attendance was sparse. The Elms is reliably rammed for internationals, and even allowing for the distressing events in Qatar, it was an uncharacteristically subdued clientele today.

I was there with my pal Tony. Tony is, to put it mildly, a proud Cardiffian and given to forthright expressions of opinion if he sees something he doesn't like. He does not like the way Wales have been playing this autumn.

'How do you think we'll do, Tone?' I ask.

'I wants us to lose,' he announces, adopting a challenging expression.

'What do you mean?'

'They'll have to sack him then, won't they?'

Now, personally, I'm constitutionally incapable of wishing a loss on Wales, but it was hard to argue with Tony's Adamstown logic. He folded his arms as Australia kicked off, then smiled and nodded as Adam Beard knocked on two seconds later.

The commitment in Wales' first half performance was heartening for those of us who actually wanted to win the game. For the first time in this campaign, there seemed to be some go-forward in contact and players were looking for work. Rio Dyer seemed determined to contribute wherever he could, popping up all over the field and taking his try beautifully.

Jac Morgan again proved himself to be a destructive ball carrier, a 'one-man wrecking machine' according to Warren Gatland. Those of us with memories recalled Wayne Pivac dropping him on the basis that he *wasn't* a strong enough ball carrier, one of countless puzzling decisions that have been made over the last couple of years.

With Wales 20 points up, the camera caught Pivac looking mightily pleased with proceedings.

'I wants him gone,' Tony reiterates, sounding like a Clifton Street version of Don Corleone.

'Shut up and drink your Diet Coke, they're playing great,' I snap.

For the next half an hour, of course, it seemed as if Wales had parked their victory at the top of a hill and left the hand brake off. Long before Australia retook the lead there was a palpable inevitability that we were going to blow this and end 2022 in turmoil. The final quarter of the game is, of course, the period in which the coach can exert direct influence and, repeating last week's decision, Pivac decided to replace a dominant scrummaging front row.

'Gone, he needs to be,' affirms Tony, as the camera returned to a now panicked-looking Welsh coaching box.

'Yep,' I concede.

For all that the WRU needs reform, and the regions need sorting out, and fans need to support the professional game, none of this can explain a national side actually achieving dominance in a match then throwing it away. In this godawful weather, and after Cymru's heartbreaking loss to Iran, Wales had a golden chance today to put a smile on the nation's face and prove that rugby remains, albeit sporadically, a source of pride. What we learned was that without Dan Biggar in the setup there is no leadership worth the name for what is obviously a talented group of players.

Emerging into slanting rain, Tony fears he hasn't made himself clear.

'They needs to sack him.'

Rats

28 May 2023

Every day's a school day and, this week, I learned that Manx shearwaters no longer nest on the Isle of Man. The favoured theory as to why these birds should have abandoned their ancestral home, which until the 1990s practiced punitive birching and criminalised homosexuality, is the Crown Dependency's intolerable population of predatory rats. 300,000 of them have undertaken the perilous journey to Skomer Island, off Pembrokeshire, which, famously, has no recent tradition of corporal punishment and operates a laissez-faire policy as regards avian refugees.

It's chastening to realise that only eight months have passed since the conclusion of Priti Patel's tenure as Home Secretary. Those warm, fuzzy days, when governance was guided by a benign belief in the goodness of humanity, seem to belong to a jumpers-for-goalposts, bicycling-spinsters nostalgic idyll when viewed from our current spot on the Tory expressway to dystopia.

When hurtling along a trajectory, it's useful to orientate yourself to a fixed point. Terrifyingly, the only stable element I can find in the UK Government is Michael Gove. In the days before Brexit kaleidoscoped politics, Mr Gove was considered to be a radical figure in David Cameron's administration. Back then, I promise younger readers I am not making this up, figures like Ken Clarke and Dominic Grieve were powerful, mainstream voices in a party whose primary appeal to voters was as a sensible, cautious vehicle for the mores of the Establishment. Their purging by Boris Johnson, who demanded Brexit-loyalty pledges from every 2019 candidate, created an entirely different Conservative Party, in which Johnson himself could be

194

considered a leftist.

Of all the lies that propelled Vote Leave to victory, the most pernicious was that Brexit was ideologically neutral. The argument ran that 'freedom' from the EU was desirable to those of all political persuasions as it would allow the UK to determine its own political course, whatever that might be. A minority on the left, such as the RMT's Mick Lynch, bought into the idea that industries would be able to argue for government subsidies that are restricted by the EU and perhaps push on to renationalisation. The overwhelming source for Vote Leave proponents, however, came from the Powellite right of the Conservative Party and beyond into the Badlands of UKIP and self-declared far-right entities like the English Defence League. For these people, immigration is a stand-alone issue, divorced from economics, let alone morality, so anti-immigration sentiments came baked into Brexit, along with the economic libertarianism of its financial backers.

In 2019, when 'getting Brexit done' was the key to a Conservative victory, Johnson, who is as ambivalent about immigration as he was about the EU before it became expedient to oppose it, looked genuinely committed to his programme of 'levelling-up'. In his mind, and that of current Levelling Up Secretary Gove, it would lead to a political realignment that would solve the Tories' dependence on elderly voters and unlock economic potential across the UK.

But it hasn't. Not here, not in the north of England, not anywhere. Yoked to a voting base that perpetually has 'legitimate concerns about immigration', the Conservatives no longer have the luxury of forward planning for the nation. All that is left for them is screeching to drown out the tolling bell of Brexit-failure. So, Braverman out-Patels Patel to convince supporters that things would be fine if only her predecessor hadn't been so soft. Gove is the last remnant of a party that believed in anything at all. Imagine that.

Parched from a never-ending economic hangover, the electorate is offered whisky to quench its thirst. Millions of jobs lie unfilled, and we are told that immigration is the worst of all ills and that the sick and disabled should instantly be retrained. Sir Keir Starmer adds a spot of water to the hooch but agrees we should 'get the numbers down'.

It occurs to me that the true danger of reinstating freedom of movement is not immigration, but emigration. The projected economic health of the UK is dire, and its persistent inequality renders swathes of it extremely hard to inhabit. Reason for leaving? Rats.

Peadar, Pints & Politics

5 February 2023

It's been a hard winter, hasn't it? A host of viruses have laid us low; we've had cold snaps, incessant rain, rampant inflation, and the return of *Love Island*. At least Warren Gatland is back though, and we can always count on the WRU to provide some uncomplicated family fun when the national serotonin level reaches minus four.

Better yet, my Irish pal Peadar, who runs the North Powys branch of Sinn Fein, has pitched up with tickets for the game. So, off we go to Porth railway station in our respective national colours, the very picture of rugby camaraderie in a divided world.

On the train, the talk turns to politics. The likelihood of Irish reunification and Welsh independence are weighed up in the crammed carriage, and by the time we reach Queen Street, a rough constitution for a Celtic league of nations has been fashioned although no agreement is reached on the administrative centre of this new player on the world stage.

Exiting Cardiff Central, we note that Central Square still suggests the aftermath of a nuclear conflict and head for the Blue Bell. This High Street hostelry used to be the Goat Major and has been my favourite pre-match venue ever since I spent an astonishing hour in the company of Basque Frenchmen who not only distributed cheese, sausage and grape skin liquor but proceeded to march around the bar in military formation singing 'Death to Spain'.

Today, however, the atmosphere is subdued. Nobody is singing and the pub is playing the sort of music enjoyed by people who dislike music.[1]

On the way to the stadium, it's noticeable that the Irish fans are in buoyant form. Never afraid to embrace a national stereotype, their green wigs and fake orange beards proliferate as we snake towards the gates and the place where our respective moods will be determined.

Anyway, in Porters afterwards we sympathise with a North Walian who had travelled down for the day and, in his misery, discovered that Liverpool had been thrashed by Wolves. His emotional banker having gone south, Peadar offered Hibernian bonhomie to the stricken soul. In short order the Celtic league of nations is back on the table as we all discover, for the second year in a row, that it's possible to become very Scottish very quickly. An England loss is the emotional equivalent of WD40, if it doesn't fix it, it can't be fixed.

Judging Cardiff Central to be too traumatic an experience, we walk up to Cathays for the train home, passing a large group of university students in matching dinner suits.

'Those bastards will be running the world soon,' Peadar observes.

We break the journey in Ponty and pop into 'spoons for a last drink. Despite the game having finished four hours ago and 12 miles away, they are taking no chances and serving drinks in plastic glasses. A teenage girl approaches Peadar and wants to buy his Ireland scarf. When no cash amount is acceptable, she offers him a lap dance for it. In terror, Peadar gives her the scarf and we head for the exit. Growing up in Derry during The Troubles is one thing but 'spoons in Ponty after a game is quite another.

---

[1] Ed Sheeran.

Abolish England!

4 June 2023

I'm not going to lie, I sorta low-key like Mark Drakeford. I mean I haven't got a tattoo of him or anything and I wouldn't want him turning up on a night out (can you imagine?), the way he talks sets my teeth on edge and I won't be voting for him, but he's OK, isn't he?

This week has seen the re-emergence of the blonde unflushable as, predictably, he attempts to use the Covid enquiry as a vehicle to ram-raid his successor in Number 10. We are collectively traumatised by the pandemic. The clearest tell for this is that nobody can remember the order in which various lockdowns, fatality spikes, and new variants occurred. A fractured timeline is typical of traumatic memories and a key reason why abuse victims are often seen as unreliable witnesses by the Crown Prosecution Service.

Whilst we often see abusers using their trial to re-traumatise their victims, I can't recall one turning up at an inquest to gaslight bereaved relatives. Boris Johnson's behaviour this week demonstrates yet again that the deaths of hundreds of thousands of UK citizens on his watch has registered as no more than a political inconvenience in what he imagines is the great sweep of his career.

In my own jumbled memories of the pandemic, Drakeford stands out for a number of reasons. Firstly, living in his shed to protect his family was leadership by example of a sort I thought was lost to UK politics. It bought the FM enough grudging respect to insist on restrictions that were crafted in his own, cautious image. Now, that was a pain in the backside at the time and history may yet record that his measures were ineffective, but during those terrifying days, most people in Wales felt that our interests were being served by a FM whose motives were unquestioned. The contrast with Westminster chaos was stark and whilst Nicola Sturgeon's performance was assured, Drakeford managed to avoid the impression that the pandemic was a political opportunity. He dished out restrictions and warnings calmly, seemingly unconcerned whether we liked him or not. It was schoolmasterly when, in truth, we all felt infantilised by a threat we could not counter.

But that was then, wasn't it? The Drakester is approaching the final furlong of his run in public life and, like all retiring politicos, his focus has shifted to 'legacy'. This seems to be a particularly Labour obsession; exiting Tories shed the responsibility of government like a despised work suit and tootle off to roll around in mountains of cash with their City pals. It's obscene, but at least we don't have to watch it. Labourites, however, have managed to convince themselves that they are the inheritors of a grand, radical tradition and, as such, duty-bound to leave their philosophical mark for future generations to pore over alongside Rousseau and Roosevelt.

The absolute king of cut-price elder statesmen is Gordon Brown. Let's recap his achievements: spent 10 years being gamed by Tony Blair, during which time he transferred responsibility for decent wages from corporations to the taxpayer; flogged off the UK gold reserves when the market was at its lowest, and failed to regulate the banks. On assuming the premiership, he dodged a winnable election just in time to see his unregulated banks tank the economy and send him into the political netherworld after calling an old lady a bigot on tape.

Since then, however, he has grown his hair out as a sure signifier that he is above the squalid dogfighting of the political class, and now projecting himself as a Merlinesque purveyor of philosophical insight into world affairs. It was in this capacity that he swept into Scotland on the eve of its independence referendum to promise last-minute concessions from the Cameron government that ensured a No vote would trigger the federalisation of the UK. As we know, this turned out to be what Brown's fellow Kirkcaldy-based free-marketeer Adam Smith might have described as 'a load of auld pish.'

It is to Brown that Mark Drakeford has hitched his wagon in a late bid to lend his career some constitutional significance. The duo are joined by Anas Sarwar, Andy Burnham and Tracy Brabin in the latest bid to persuade unionists and separatists that a third way is possible. First off, having Brown head this up is like handing Phil Mitchell the keys to the Vic in the expectation that he'll turn it into a vegan chai house. Cut Gordon open and he'd bleed green leather and order papers, he is a Westminster politician to his marrow.

The opening statement from the 'Alliance for Radical Democratic Change' (!) falls apart on contact with the air. In paragraph one they seek to, 'devolve effective economic and social powers to the regions and nations.' Just two paragraphs later the relevance-hungry has-beens reckon they can deliver 'a union which offers strong devolution for all parts of the UK; a union where all four nations are treated as equals.'

Now, I'm not a mathematician, but given that the population of England is 56 million, whilst there are 3.1 million of us here in Wales, I'd conclude that any federal arrangement that leaves England intact as a political entity has domination of the smaller nations baked into it.

As someone who grew up in Birmingham, I'd like to help them out with their evident confusion. England doesn't exist in any meaningful way and should be abolished.

If you travel to the Black Country, or Yorkshire, Lancashire, Devon, East Anglia, or anywhere else that labours under the false cloak of Englishness, you'll find distinct accents, dialects, food, senses of humour, ways of greeting and socio-political mores that denote the existence of living, breathing cultures. It is impossible not to be charmed by the absurdist humour you find in Dudley, or the spectacular delicacies of Lancashire, or the always-great music in Manchester. These cultures thrive in the words and deeds of living humans whose joys and sorrows find expression through them. What, on the other hand, is Englishness? It is impossible to conceive of it without deferring to a received history that paid attention only to the ruling class. Its claimed characteristics: the 'stiff upper lip', stoicism, and deference are the virtues of serfs whose obligation is to keep quiet in the face of unjust rule. 'Keep Calm and Carry On', as those T-shirts bearing the crown urge.

The flag of St George has magical powers. The regions east of Wales have birthed a universe of radical ideas, inventions, and art, but once draped in the red cross all of that is silenced in a way that the Union flag could never mute the Celtic nations. The shameful scenes attached to England football supporters over the years speak of an ugly nationalism that is rooted in insecurity and a childlike craving for discipline. Englishness diminishes a diverse group of people to a powerless mob whose status is defined from above. Regional identities sing in their own voices, Englishness bellows its masters' orders.

So, Mr Drakeford, if you are serious about federalisation, let's get real about what that entails. There can be no equality of nations if one of them is an artificial superstate with a fabricated culture that serves solely to preserve the political status quo. Unless the people of the regions of England wake up to their own disadvantage within it then the English 'nation' will remain grotesquely overpowered in any federal settlement.

As I began writing this piece, news came through that the popular Mayor of North of Tyne, Jamie Driscoll, has been barred by Keir Starmer's Labour from running for the expanded role of North East Mayor that will replace his office. Anybody placing faith in the Labour Party to decentralise the UK shouldn't hold their breath.

1

---

[1] The title of this piece won me dozens of Scottish Twitter followers.

On Raglan Road

19 March 2023

This Six Nations has been different, hasn't it? We've had bad years before, and some of them far worse than this as regards performances on the pitch. Never before, though, has it felt as if the whole shooting match was slipping from our grasp. A bad year used to mean a change of coach or a switch-up in selection, this year we've watched the games unfold in the knowledge that Welsh rugby is under an urgent, existential threat.

For those of us who love this game and what it means to Wales, the last few months have been traumatic. That's an overused word but in this instance, I employ it with confidence, because rugby has mattered to this nation, and at times mattered a great deal.

I watched the game in Raglan, where the landscape has no jagged edges and independent businesses enjoy a backwash from the English economy. Burgers are £14.95, cash preferred according to the sign on the wall.

The opposite of love isn't hatred, but disinterest, and nobody in the pub was particularly bothered when the signal on the TV kept failing, even when it deprived us of the first Welsh try during an opening 20 minutes that might have offered hope to supporters who didn't know better.

We were joined by a boy of about 10 whose family were eating in the other room. He'd abandoned his lunch to watch the match and had an edgy intensity that will be familiar to any of you who have watched games through your fingers as if your life is at stake.

For a brief while, watching him follow the play was a joy.

203

He'd already developed the habit of talking out loud to players and the referee as if he were stood next to them, for no reason other than to give life to his informed opinions. Then he was joined by his dad.

Dad's opening line was,

'7-7, well they're two very well-matched teams.'

I noticed the boy's lips purse at this and tuned in as the conversation developed.

'So, this stadium is called Parc des Princes, son. That means Park of the Princes.'

'No, it isn't, it's the Stade de France; Stade Francais play there.'

'Oh yes, that's right, they changed it didn't they. It's the national stadium, though, no club teams play there, they couldn't get the crowds to fill it.'

The boy was batting this away whilst maintaining rapt attention on the game, correctly calling offside decisions and pre-empting the touch judge's concerns about illegal tackles. Dad carried on.

'It's just silly to think that a club would play at the national stadium, that's reserved for international games.'

As the second quarter began to reveal Wales' deficiencies, his son's patience was stretched.

'Just look it up when you get home,' he snapped.

I hadn't allowed my own heartbeat to raise by so much as a semi-quaver during the closely contested early exchanges. Wales were obviously going to lose this game and the older you get the more parsimonious you become with the investment of your remaining stores of hope.

As we were overrun in the opening minutes of the second half, the rest of the boy's family came to collect him and dad, raving about the waffles they had missed out on for dessert. Dad clowned with his daughter's ear muffs and the boy was dragged reluctantly away, looking behind him at the screen as if some miracle might occur if he willed it.

In the Doghouse

Finally, when there was no other choice, he got a big decision right. Spitting denials and venom, Boris Johnson was propelled out of public life like a spoiled dog who has soiled the rug once too often. His bared teeth at Rishi Sunak put us on notice, as if we needed it, that we haven't heard the last of a man whose estimation of his own virtues is exceeded only by his capacity for self-deception. When you've been World King since you were six, you don't abdicate because the courtiers have got a bit uppity. You regroup and come again.

Johnson is 'bewildered and appalled' that Parliament could treat him like this. Since school he's had to contend with no-talent mediocrities trying to damp down the fizz of his brilliance in the service of their paltry, bureaucratic ambitions and this is no different. Go on holiday, make a few quid, charm the public then wreak revenge. They'll see.

And you wouldn't put it past him, would you? Give it six months of Keir Starmer droning on about how we can't afford anything and who's to say the country won't be better disposed towards a party-hard attitude? Press one for a depressed-looking bloke with a quiff explaining that global instability precludes a reappraisal of marginal tax rates, or two for a bastard on a zipwire waving flags.

The 'big dog' inveigling his way out of the kennel and back on to the sofa is a scenario that should shock nobody at this point. The current performative moralising of the political class about Johnson's misdeeds belies the plain fact that nobody stopped him doing anything he liked until he became politically inconvenient. Commentators and politicians tutted away impotently whilst people like Nazanin Zaghari-Ratcliffe were thrown under the lovely London bus of Johnson's career. Remember the model bus interview?

By the time he became PM, Johnson was so comfortable lying to the nation that he felt able to do it for giggles. A persona that was reputedly forged during a school play, when he realised he was getting laughs for forgetting his lines, became a template for governing the UK during its most turbulent period since World War Two. Nobody who mattered stood up during the pandemic and demanded that he be removed as a matter of national safety. As the bodies piled up, he was permitted to carry on winging it regardless of the consequences, and the failure of our system to cut him down when the stakes were highest is a stark indicator of how dysfunctional it is.

We're now to be subjected to Johnson's pose as a man of the people who has been wronged by an elite 'blob' that controls both major parties and the Civil Service. When your entire career is founded upon opportunistic dishonesty, there is no option but to pile on the lies when you come under fire. He can't rest upon his achievements, nor can he take refuge in any consistent principles that might explain his opponents' desire to see him fall. Johnson's only defence is to make the lie bigger and more wide-ranging. Where once it was 'Remoaners' who were blocking him and, by extension, the 'will of the people', now it is a conspiracy that extends into every institutional body in the land. In the expensively furnished Johnson bunker, the fortunes of the nation are indivisible from his personal wellbeing and if he's at his lowest ebb, so must be the nation. His pain is our pain.

When Donald Trump said he could shoot someone on Fifth Avenue and still see his numbers go up, he touched the zeitgeist with chilling accuracy. If a politician's rhetoric is divisive enough, then his popularity thrives not despite his misdeeds but because of them. An occasional dogwhistling nod to base prejudices, like blithely characterising niqab-wearers as 'letter boxes', is enough to alert your fans that you are one of them.

Nothing is more psychologically powerful than legitimising the taboo, because in liberating people from their shame at subscribing to societally proscribed beliefs you possess their wellbeing, and come to embody it.

The professional rapscallion, Mizzy, has recently had the nation clutching its pearls in horror as he monetises everything from breaking and entering to dog theft in TikTok videos. Wearing his cheeky psychopathy lightly, he reels off his viewing stats as de facto justification for his content. People watch it therefore it is good. I wasn't above a spot of mindless vandalism myself as a youth, less so nowadays on account of my bad back, and we can agree that obnoxious teenagers are nothing new. What has changed, though, is the context for his behaviour. When I was lobbing a brick through a window, I did it in the sure knowledge that the entire hierarchy of adult society disapproved of what I was doing. When Mizzy pranks someone, it's in a world where a guy who reckons being famous means you can grab any bit of a woman you like can become President of the USA. Outrage the nation, get invited on Piers Morgan to be shouted at, watch your views go up.

Trump and Johnson offer a blueprint as to how politics works in a moral vacuum. In exile, the former PM will be denuded of the fig leaf of civic responsibility so free to lob bombs into the public space and bask in their incendiary results. No matter how hard we wish it, the world isn't going back to the 1990s and if we don't want it to belong to malevolent narcissists then we need to find some leaders who understand its new mechanics. As Joe Biden stumbles towards a second presidential election, and Keir Starmer abandons substantive policies in the name of caution, it's hard to believe that they represent any kind of lasting reset. Politicians need to find a way to feed principles into algorithms effectively, or Mizzy for PM lies on the horizon.

Cometh the Hour, Cometh the Liar

18 June 2023

There was a grim inevitability to Boris Johnson's governmental adventure concluding with him and Nadine Dorries emerging into a hail of bullets like Butch Cassidy and the Sundance Kid. The only mystery is why the gods took so long to be angered by a display of hubris that made Louis XIV look like John Major. I suspect that, like the rest of us, they were paralysed in rapt disbelief that such a character was being permitted to cavort on the world stage at all. It was a thing to watch, you can't deny.

A clue as to how he got away with it for so long lies with the craven invertebrates he leaves behind in Westminster. Rishi Sunak, who seems to view the premiership as a sort of gap-year volunteering placement before returning to a proper job in 'tech', didn't see fit to comment on the Privileges Committee report at all. He knows right well that his former boss can spill the beans on him whenever he likes, and one can picture him anxiously refreshing the *Daily Mail*'s website to see what Johnson's first column had in store. That it turned out to be a genial lifestyle piece on slimming can only have prolonged his suffering. He's food.

Further down the menu, the collective 'I always knew he was a wrong-un' mumbling from Parliamentary also-rans who were happy enough to 'back Boris' when there were still votes in it dignifies nobody. Tory MPs never tire of telling us how their policies reward 'risk-takers' who create wealth for the country. How telling that they should wait until Johnson's head has been spiked in Parliament Square before venturing an ounce of their own political fortunes on such an outcome.

We are already being told that we want to 'move on' from

the Johnson affair. In a week or so any mention of it will be met with eye-rolling sighs as if it were a non-event that's only of interest to embittered obsessives with an agenda. You've seen this manoeuvre before when we were told we wanted to move on from Brexit, Grenfel, Covid etc. etc. etc. We are encouraged to view each of these calamities as stand-alone misfortunes rather than a narrative arc of incompetence and malfeasance. In this instance, the convenient take is to ascribe the entire business to Johnson alone, as if his dishonesty was an aberration of which we have now been rid.

I put it to you that Johnson was, and remains, the perfect standard bearer for the United Kingdom in the 21st Century.

Take a look around you at the deserted, hollowed-out town centres, the potholed roads, the years' long waiting lists for medical treatment, the food banks, the falling life expectancy, the endemic mental health problems, the skills shortages...

We're not going through a bad patch; all of this is the logical result for a country that has been ruined by crackpot economics and straightforward larceny for decades. Kept afloat on a sea of debt, we have seen our industrial base, in other words our *usefulness*, decimated in favour of a financial services industry whose profits spread no further than the Home Counties. The rest of us either scrap over the bones of it or prosper via the artificial inflation of house prices in a Ponzi scheme that has left our young people at the mercy of an increasingly venal rentier class.

All of this has been obvious for most of my adult life but rather than address it, our leaders, and we allow it whether we voted for them or not, have offered up toxic patriotism, xenophobia, and bullying of the disadvantaged as displaced channels for the nation's unhappiness.

The unhinged self-mutilation of Brexit isn't the cause of our woes, it's the latest and grandest event in a long tradition of self-deception.

I was in the pub one afternoon (yeah, I know), when a bloke pitched up in white Gucci loafers and plenty of gold jewellery. He stood at the bar having a pint and making sure everyone noticed him before leaving in a haze of Paco Rabane cologne.

An old boy in the corner looked up from his newspaper and observed,'

'Thousand pound millionaire.'

'What do you mean?' asked the landlord.

'Merc on the drive and f*ck all in the fridge.'

That's where the UK is as a nation. Wheeling out Charles in a golden coach to receive the baubles of an empire none of us can remember, the Sceptred Isle is all fur coat and no knickers.

There's only so many tears in the social fabric that you can patch up with Union flags before it disintegrates and reveals the Great British sham in all its decrepitude. Boris Johnson wasn't a uniquely dishonest Prime Minister; he was the Prime Minister of a uniquely dishonest country. His blustering appeal to a supposed former greatness echoed round the derelict ruins of post-industrial Britain like a hospital radio jingle.

It's ironic that the UK's attachment to the lies of empire should prove to be its undoing as former colonies surge past it towards prosperity. As the death throes of the old bulldog find voice in Johnson's outrage at being removed as Bullshitter in Chief, Scotland, Northern Ireland, and Wales should take stock. Project UK isn't getting better any time soon.

The Week in Depth

25 June 2023

When I started off doing this column, I sacrificed reading Marina Hyde in *The Guardian* on the basis that she's so good I'd want to steal from her.[1] Boris Johnson's new column in the *Daily Mail* presents a rather different problem, in that it explicitly begs to be ripped apart and is designed that way. Rather like the animal that wanted to be eaten in *The Hitchhiker's Guide to the Galaxy*, it's an opinion piece that wants you to disagree with it. So, I won't. Well maybe this one time, then I'll never mention it again. It'll go on the *verboten* pile alongside Marina, *Question Time*, and *Lord of the Rings*, each of which I deem taboo, but for diverse reasons too revealing to discuss with you. At least, not yet.

This week, he holds forth on the submarine implosion. Now, it doesn't matter what he actually says (really, it doesn't, trust me on this one) but his choice of subject throws up the central question about him: to what extent is he taking the piss? I can see only two conclusions one can draw from his article. Either the pseudo-patriotic, 'proud to be British' piffle he's knocked out this week reveals him as a proper simpleton rather than a pretend one, or he's so keen to wear the disapproval of left-wing journos that he's willing to write their lines for them. Because, if you can't fashion a longform metaphor out of an imploded submarine and Boris Johnson, then you're in the wrong job. Let's see how many writers take the bait…

Anyway, the submarine. These types of events create a strange national space. In 'mesmerised horror' as *Black Mirror* has it, we're all looking at the same thing, for once, and it's

---

[1] True facts. It is impossible to write anything original with her golden phrases rattling around your head.

invoking something we usually experience privately: the fear of death. Don't tell me, you're 'not afraid of death, only of dying'. Chinny reckon[2]. Bullishness is a respectable coping strategy for terror, but let's not pretend it's anything more. Avoidance is another psychological tic we develop to keep the show on the road when it all gets a bit existential, and we've all had plenty of that flashing across our socials this week. We've had Marxist avoidance, in which the wealth of those in jeopardy outweighs the jeopardy itself and becomes the new focus; scientific avoidance, whereby we geek out on the tech and oceanography; and the more conventional 'I don't care about it because lots of people die all the time' sort that my WWII-era Gran used to favour: 'I don't understand why these oldies are all going on about hypothermia, it's a very peaceful death. I'm 92 and I'd be *delighted* if that's the way I go!'

As much as anything, you've got to feel for scientists the world over. Since the pandemic, when the cream of the world's boffins offered us paper hankies with ear straps as our salvation, they've taken a bit of a knock in public affections. Finding the sub would have gone some way to restoring their reputation as regards arse/elbow differentiation capabilities but, sadly, it was not to be.

The sea, it turns out, is bigger than you might imagine. To compound matters, it apparently gets quite dark towards the bottom; so much so that the fish down there don't have eyes! If they possessed ocular organs, they'd no doubt raise a slimy eyebrow at the arrival, at their depth, of a vessel manufactured out of titanium *and* carbon fibre.

'Surely the seam point between two materials of differing resilience must be a weakness against the mindboggling number of units of force per square centimetre down here?' they'd say.

---

[2] If you have to look this up, I guarantee you have never owned a Raleigh Grifter, nor shed a tear for Kurt Cobain.

It's highly unlikely that anyone would hear them, though.

Before it became clear that the loss of the sub was due to a mercifully brief incident, we all imagined ourselves in the doomed craft and wondered how we'd behave. *Would I be Captain Oatesish?* With mortality having a rare turn in the public sphere, we experienced its weapon, time, in all its awful splendour. When lives are at stake, time transforms from the chugging meter of hours, days and weeks into something that accelerates and decelerates simultaneously, hurtling us in slow motion towards an outcome.

I'm sure there's a scientific explanation for this phenomenon and I'm sure that there's another one that directly contradicts it in a peer reviewed article. Which is the problem with science. While it has a great track record of preventing or causing deaths, it's very sketchy on certainties we can cling to when we're faced with them. The 'hill in the distance' that Larkin described casts its shadow on us all and how we cope with its perpetual presence defines our characters.

So, when a small, imaginable group of people, whose faces we have seen, are thought to be trapped in the face of oblivion, we reach for our crutches and hobble through the ordeal with them. *Not like that* we plead, whether to our God or the cat.

Pulled Back In

6 August 2023

Unexpected good mood!

I nearly didn't go out to see the game. I was *supposed* to watch it in Swansea, but apocalyptic weather warnings put paid to that trip. So, it was either an isolated ordeal at home in front of Amazon Prime (Grrrr) or go somewhere local to take my medicine. It was a close decision. We've all been through some times watching Wales: the fall from grace in the 1980s, the traumatic hellscape of the 1990s, Western Samoa, Fiji, Western Samoa again, Italy, Georgia for heaven's sake. It always felt as if things could be righted, though. New tactics, a change of coach or a talented youngster breaking through were all Wales needed to keep our hopes afloat.

This year has been different. Chaos at the WRU and the exodus of so many players to foreign clubs made the chill of defeat in the Six Nations seem more like climate change than another patch of bad weather.

International football days in Cardiff saw the city flooded with a bucket-hatted joy that celebrated the nation with abandon win or lose. To remain committed to rugby, with its endless bickering, offensive, antiquated management and three *blydi* feathers, began to feel like clinging to the corpse of a cherished relative. No fun. No fun at all.

Misery loves company, though, so I trooped down to the club in Ynyshir braced for the worst. There were a decent few in by kick-off but it was subdued, no jerseys being worn, nobody discussing the game. The anthem was observed quietly but without the rapt anticipation that accompanies it in the good

215

times.

Perversely, I felt rather better about it than has been the case recently. Settling down with a drink, as the sun peeped through the window, I realised there was no knot in my stomach. *Have I died?* I wondered. After checking my vital signs, it seemed I was still clogging up the physical realm but experiencing the heady freedom of hopelessness. The gnawing hunger for Welsh success had been replaced by a Zen acceptance that the events would unfold as they would: the Wayne Pivac path to enlightenment.

The second Gatland era seemed destined for disaster. Aside from the catastrophic infrastructure collapse of the game in Wales, there was a distinct impression that he was only here for the money. Twitter was full of discontent at the great man's extracurricular appointments at the opening of shops and the like, whilst some pointed to out-of-date tactics during the Six Nations and his failure to make a clear statement about the misogynism scandal that enveloped the WRU shortly after his appointment. *Was his heart really in it?*

Over the last week, Gatland seemed uncharacteristically optimistic about his squad's prospects. After his traditional pre-World Cup beasting, this time in Switzerland, the players enjoyed a positive reaction from their coach in interviews.

'I'm really excited. I'm telling you this team will do something pretty special,' he gushed on Wednesday.

There were clear signs of progress in the first half. While England looked muscular in contact, Wales were organising well and demonstrating good basic skills under pressure. England's three-point lead at half-time owed much to the preening referee's invention of a new law preventing a player having a ball thrown at his stationery hand, and hopeless gullibility as regards front row gamesmanship at the scrum.

Heading out for a vape into the miracle Rhondda sunshine – again *have I died?* – I was still calmly sure that we'd lose. *20 points shipped in the first 15 minutes,* I silently predicted, all too familiar with sluggish second-half openings that prove irretrievable.

But no. With Jac Morgan rampant as captain, this Wales team began to look like a proper handful. Gaining supremacy in contact, they were unafraid to go wide and, wonder of wonders, seemed to have rediscovered how to defend.

When Rio Dyer missed a tackle in the first half, Steffan, at the next table, groaned,

'Dyer Straits!'

Dyer missed another one in the second period but leapt to his feet, chased down his man and scragged him. Steffan turned to me and grinned.

It was warming up in the club, with all eyes on the screen and the ref copping for some choice language when he privileged a millimetre of air over Rees-Zammit's magnificent try.

The World Cup just might be something to look forward to and enjoy.

Walking home, I was reminded of that line in *The Sopranos.*[1]

'Just when I thought I was out, they pull me back in...'

---

[1] A reader pointed out that this was actually from *The Godfather: Part III.* Fortunately, my editor was on hand to educate him that the line had been quoted in an episode of *The Sopranos*, before screenshotting his impudent comment and sending it to his employers.

Last of the Summer Whine

2 July 2023

However ground down and spiritually impoverished you have been by the UK political scene over the last few years, I warn you that the forthcoming General Election will require accessing reserves of moral fibre generally earmarked for palliative self-care.

We know the grim territory that the Tories will choose to die on: refugees and gender issues.

'Mr Sunak, with a loaf of bread now costing £8.75, what fiscal strategies do you propose to help people put food on the table?'

'Laura, I've been very clear that my pledge is to cut inflation. I'm sure that you guys in the electorate understand that the real question is whether an inflatable dinghy can have a penis. I say it can't, what does Captain Flip-Flop say?'

So far, so predictable, the flailing demise of a bankrupt government can be an enjoyable spectacle when a healthy democracy corrects course and changes personnel. The model for this is 1997, when John Major's disintegrating party was swept away on a tide of New Labour modernity. The old yielded to the new as naturally as the turning of the seasons and we looked forward to a new millennium full of ciabatta and public/private partnerships.

Fast-forward to today, and Labour has none of the confidence that fuelled the Blair landslide. Bold signature policies like the minimum wage and child tax credits have been replaced by obsessive cautiousness and a commitment not to worry the bond markets.

Part of the problem lies in the decline in moral authority with which Labour now wrestles. Soon after coming to power, Blair went on TV to explain why Formula One, owned by Labour donor Bernie Ecclestone, had been excluded from the ban on tobacco advertising ban in sport.

'I think most people recognise me as a pretty straight guy,' Blair beamed, expending the first few coins of political capital that would eventually be exhausted by the Iraq War.

When evaluating the Blair/Brown years, it's tempting for the political class to compare them favourably to the austerity-blighted, Brexity, Covidy quagmire that we've endured since. The problem with this reading is that if the New Labour government had done what it said on the tin, then the mechanics of wealth distribution would have been tooled to ensure that the nations and regions of the UK weren't so economically hollowed out by globalisation that their voters were prone to exploitation by faux-nationalist con artists like Nigel Farage.

So don't expect Keir Starmer to barnstorm around Britain in a euphoric seizure of the political zeitgeist. Whilst Boris Johnson was being cast into the desert the other week, Shadow Chancellor Rachel Reeves quietly announced that Labour would be continuing with the triple lock on pensions. You will find no economist who supports this policy, so she defended it on moral grounds as the 'right thing to do'. Labour pledges no longer deemed feasible include commitments to abolish tuition fees, invest in green energy and nationalise utilities so, whilst the CEO of Saga Cruises sighs with relief, the rest of us are facing another election in which the voting intentions of the elderly is the only game in town. I'm not suggesting that the gerontocracy should be stripped of their franchise, of course I'm not, nobody could accuse me of that and if you infer it then that says more about you than I, who never thought such a thing. There is a smidge of a problem though, I think, with large and crucial voting blocks being decades past their experience of the workplace, which is where much of people's offline political engagement occurs. At

219

work, you must put up with other people's abhorrent or asinine political views and maintain a relationship. If you air your own startling take on the issues of the day, you need to be able to defend it against people whose only commonality with you is use of the same car park.

In retirement, we no longer have to listen to Sue from Accounts explaining why she'd bring back the birch or Dave the Stock Controller insisting that climate change is a Globalist plot. The trouble is that while you are looking forward to a retirement characterised by philosophical reflection on the human condition, Dave and Sue will also have time on their hands and Twitter feeds where every post they see agrees with them. Without you to issue corrective lectures in the canteen, they are at the mercy of the algorithm, and there lie trolls repeating the dog whistles of GB News 24 hours a day.

The most depressing aspect of this scenario is that the ludicrous generalisations I've just made about older voters are no more offensive than the assumptions of the major parties. Both Labour and the Tories insist that immigration must come down as a general principle, despite an acute labour shortage across the UK. Neither will ascribe our ills to Brexit, in the face of mounting evidence that it is leading to ruin, and enthusiastic participation in confected culture wars is standard across the board.

The election is set to be pitched at imaginary voters whom politicians believe to be mean-minded, credulous, and regressive. Dreaming up an electorate fashioned in their own image is only going to work for as long as it takes for actual voters to give up on them and seek valid representation. On current form, that day can't be far off.

The Kingdom of Bevan

9 July 2023

Britain officially moved on from the pandemic this week when journalistic shills for high finance resumed their calls for a 'grown-up conversation' about the NHS.

'Don't you think it's a bit weird they are having a religious service for a government service?'

tweeted the GB News, Talk TV, *Telegraph, Spectator, Mail* mouthpieces, in unison as if guided by the common unconscious. The likelihood of complex thinkers like Darren Grimes, Michelle Dewberry, and the rest having the same thought *at the same time* seems remote, but when you're wired to the zeitgeist like these guys, strange shit can happen.

The NHS, we are told, is inefficient because our emotional attachment to it prevents reform. We treat our health system as a 'quasi-religion' – a 'sacred cow' about which even the discussion of change is taboo. Well, yes actually, we do. As we are feasted on by private utilities companies and parasitical government contract holders, we know right well that Béarnaise sauce awaits cows whose sanctity is voted away.

The genius of neoliberal politics has been to discredit principles in the face of utilitarianism. It is no longer sufficient to object to anything on the basis that it is morally wrong. Before the ethics of an issue can be addressed, we are expected to win on cost-analysis alone. The mechanics of this are simple: if something is allowed to fall into chaos then a short-term injection of private capital will always look attractive, as long as the long-term social cost is excluded from the analysis. In this way, we are persuaded that objecting to private finance in our healthcare system is privileging political dogma at the expense of new equipment, buildings, and higher wages.

So, let's clear that hurdle with three words. The. Water. Industry.

Everyone clear about that? Good, we'll move on.

The principled argument for healthcare being wholly publicly funded is that illness is not a commodity. When we own the system, we are incentivised to minimise illness because it costs us. Public health initiatives make sense in a public system as a healthier population benefits all. Illness is, as Nye Bevan had it, a *misfortune*. Once a profit motive is introduced into the system, your ingrowing toenail ceases to be a misfortune and becomes an opportunity. Pharmaceutical companies, of course, already operate on this model but are, at least, subject to the clinical decisions of NHS doctors. The private road leads, eventually, to outrages like the OxyContin scandal in the USA.

Apologists for public/private partnerships and outsourcing object to the use of American examples. Preferring to point to more equitable shared cost schemes in Europe, they insist that nobody is suggesting that we adopt the American model. Well, I'm loath to repeat myself, but the rebuttal to that is:

The. Water. Industry.

What, after the experience of the last forty years, could possibly persuade you that a privately run service in the UK would act in a uniquely ethical fashion, tempering its pursuit of profit for the greater good? Are our privately run trains cheaper and more efficient than those in Europe? Do we enjoy insulation from price spikes courtesy of our private utilities companies? Are our privately run prisons models of rehabilitation? Anybody trusting the cheerleaders of private enterprise to give a gnat's chuff about healthcare outcomes for those without means should make their case waist-deep in a polluted river or from an excrement-strewn beach.

I am not religious but would willingly convert to any faith that guarantees Tony Blair's reckoning before a just deity. To mark the 75th birthday of the NHS, his organisation released a report that suggested people should be allowed to pay for expedited NHS treatment. Like you[1], it escapes me how a man with the Iraq War in his CV is permitted a platform on which to lecture us, but there he is so let's engage. Somewhere between 1997 Tony, the people-pleasing validation sponge who promised a way out of Thatcherism, and 2023 Tony, the peevish Admonisher-In-Chief, he's conveniently forgotten that the improvement in NHS performance on his watch was built on solid public funding. It rose from 3% of government spending under Thatcher/Major to 6% under Blair/Brown, before plummeting to 1% under Cameron. It's now at 1.7%, with the Tories offering a rise to 3%. Keir Starmer's offer would see it come in at just under 4%.

Whatever effects, good or bad, that New Labour's public/private partnerships had can only be viewed in the context of unprecedented public funding of the service. If the NHS were The Beatles' *Abbey Road*, public/private partnerships were 'Octopus's Garden' by Ringo.

The figures show that Keir Starmer's new New Labour has swallowed Blair's revisionism and believes that restoring funding to below that offered by the Thatcher government will suffice, presumably if accompanied by 'reform'. When an underfunded service continues not to improve, the prescription will be for yet more 'reform' until the original form is unrecognisable.

The NHS was not born in Labour Party think tanks, but in Tredegar where it operated in micro form long before its MP took it to the wider UK. The UK Labour Party's ownership of the concept is a fraud and politicians of the left here in Wales should

---

[1] This is deliberate provocation. Seeming to assume that everyone agrees with me boils the piss of regular critics who have been known to write comments that are longer than the article with which they disagree. It's good, clean fun.

be drawing a bold distinction between how we view the institution as opposed to the hybrid, deconstructed version favoured by the servile opposition in Westminster.

For all the opaque, economic theorising of Blair and his successors, the choice remains simple: shareholders either profit from our misfortune, or they don't.

Meeja Studies

16 July 2023

Sad news this week when it emerged that George Armstrong, who played Alan Humphries in the original run of *Grange Hill*, had passed away, aged 60. For the benefit of readers not of the Greatest Generation, if you meet a British Gen X'r who says they didn't watch *Grange Hill* as a kid then they are a wrong 'un and you should make your excuses and leave. It was, you see, a defining cultural product of the late '70s and early '80s. Uniquely for children's TV of the time, its leading characters were overtly transgressive. Tucker Jenkins: part Artful Dodger, part James Dean, severed forever the connection between virtue and being well-behaved. Girls wanted him, boys wanted to be him. I remember being discomfited when Todd Carty took the role of Mark Fowler in *Eastenders*, fearing that associating him with another character might undermine the authenticity of Tucker, whom a part of me believed still existed somewhere in the world. Fortunately, the understated range of Carty's craft resolved that issue.

As the show progressed, female characters came to the fore, showcasing a righteous chippiness that seems a world away from the infantilised, faux rebellion of '90s Girl Power. The queen of no-fucks-given classroom youthitude[1] was Suzanne Ross, played by Susan Tully who went on to play Mark's sister, Michelle, in *Eastenders*.

Peace was never an option for Suzanne when it came to teachers. Her inexhaustible appetite for conflict gave voice to a generation who were contending with Boomerdom at its most

---

[1] © B. Wildsmith 2023.

distressingly self-confident stage. Imagine Alan Sugar[2] when he still had lead in his pencil and you get a sense of how swaggering the adult world seemed at the time. Suzanne believed that the curriculum should reflect changes in how the world worked and the one line I retain from *Grange Hill* scripts was her urgently delivered,

'I wanna do Meeja Studies!'

In retrospect, it's clear that this zeitgeist-invoking plea was an early tell for the collapse of civilization that we are now experiencing.

Marshall McLuhan told us that 'The medium is the message' in 1964 and it took 20 years to percolate down from academia, through business to fictional schoolkids. Politicians, typically, were slower to catch on which accounts for Tony Blair's double-glazing-salesman-with-a-conscience schtick seeming so slick in 1997. Prior to this, media training for politicians had been limited to someone asking Maggie Thatcher to tone down the screeching a bit. When post-war social mobility emboldened the electorate to demand accountability from the ruling class, the media assumed an importance in British life that would have been unthinkable in the black & white recent past.

In this 1951 interview with Anthony Eden, Leslie Mitchell demonstrates the cringing deference then required by politicians of the press.

Good evening. I would just like to say that, as an interviewer, and as I what I hope you will believe to be an unbiased member of the electorate, I'm most grateful to Mr Anthony Eden for inviting me to cross-question him on the present political issues ... Well now, Mr Eden, with your very considerable experience of foreign affairs, it's quite obvious that I should start by asking you

---

[2] Every time he is on telly, I remember the Amstrad boombox I got for my 11th birthday that fell apart after two weeks. His ennoblement is emblematic of all that has ensued since.

something about the international situation today, or perhaps you would prefer to talk about home. Which is it to be?

By the time Suzanne was demanding Media Studies, the power balance had reversed as newspaper corporations and TV news treated politicians like office juniors who had broken the photocopier. With Rupert Murdoch seemingly empowered to install and remove prime ministers, her insistence was reasonable.

Big-time media has a power so encompassing that we have ceased to notice it in operation. It shapes our politics with elemental inevitability, as if 'scandals', 'gaffes', and 'U-Turns' were as real as the weather, instead of journalistic tropes to attract eyeballs.

If you take a step back from TV news presentations and assess them objectively, they are sensationally weird. The futuristic sets, swooping camera work, expensive hair-dos and portentous, but deeply camp music lend an ersatz importance to something that occurs every day at 6 p.m. whether anything has happened or not.

There's a sense that those involved in broadcast news breathe their own ozone. Their relationship with government seems to be dysfunctionally close yet abusive: a symbiotic race to the bottom characterised by toxic gossip and fake outrage.

The preening self-regard, hubris, and detachment inherent to modern TV news renders it vulnerable to evisceration at the hands of the mob, and the mob has Twitter accounts. Just as the press duffed up the aristocratic political scene after the war, the sans-culottes of internet and cable TV news are at the throats of the establishment media. Or so they would have you believe.

In reality, the free-speech warriors of GB News are backed by international finance, whilst Talk TV is the latest head on the Murdoch hydra. Their practice involves persuading their viewers to ignore perilous and worsening conditions by telling them what they want to hear. Here's presenter Darren Grimes, a real person not a Dickens character, reassuring them on climate change.

'Don't go on holiday, it's too hot. Oh? I was hoping to jet off to southern Europe to be colder than a witch's tit. I mean honestly, it's the height of summer, of course it's hot. They're treating us like kids, seeking to infantilise and terrify us into backing their net zero con.'

That's cheerful, isn't it? Far more palatable than having to hear how Cardiff will be a lake at some unspecified time in the future. It's simple, it's common sense and it's what real people think but are afraid to say. Hey, you know what else real people think? That tax cuts for the rich strengthen the economy. Thanks Darren.

The model is different for these outlets. They only need to speak to potential customers and are therefore unshackled from the contending narratives that must be accommodated by the main broadcasters. That allows them to wage asymmetrical war on a 'mainstream media' that, perversely, is mandated to include their side of the confected argument in an act of institutional self-flagellation. With organisations profiting from persuading a section of the public that traditional news sources are corrupt, it should come as no surprise that the public faces of broadcast news are frequently *becoming* the news.

When Angus Deayton had his indiscretions splashed across the press, producers at *Have I Got News For You* realised the potential for ruin in a single presenter and replaced him with a changing cast of guests. ITV and the BBC should reflect that allowing what's presented as an attempt at objectivity to be fronted by a handful of instantly recognisable millionaires is asking for trouble. If one of them is disgraced, their identification with the message becomes poisonous. Informing the public of tragic news in a respectful, soothing way is a skill, for sure, but the ability to do it shouldn't be valued above the news itself.

Emotional Weather

13 August 2023

God help us all, it matters again. Watching Wales over the last couple of years has been a queasy experience. As failures on and off the pitch spiralled into a bankruptcy of hope, disappointment gave way to anger, depression, and, eventually, a resigned apathy that seemed to threaten the game's place in the national consciousness. The eight-year-old within all of us, who believed that one day he or she might pull on the red jersey, was grown jaded by experience.

A narrative of decline suggested that the national side's woes were the wages of decades long mismanagement of the game at large. If you thought about it for too long, you could extrapolate that line of thought into life in general. Perhaps the malaise was emblematic of a way of life that couldn't cut it in an efficiency-obsessed world where computers decide everything and wing threequarters have to be 8'2".

The emotional weather here, however, is as febrile as the elements. Driving up Rhondda Fawr yesterday morning towards the Rhigos, the rain drowned out the radio at times before giving way to snatches of bright, teasing sun. Plenty of jerseys were being worn to the shops. I'd considered my own XXXL relic, sadly deciding it was an X short.[1] A column of lads barrelled down Treorchy High Street in pretty dresses and green wigs, beers aloft, as you do. Two girls held a conversation from either side of a pedestrian crossing, improvising sign language when they couldn't be heard.

---

[1] This is a lie. I've actually lost four stone but pretend to be more overweight than I am in the hope that it insulates me from accusations of preening self-regard.

229

Over the Beacons, drenched sheep stared at us as if we could turn off the rain. *Do something*, they implored. A group of ponies huddled together in muttering stoicism. At Pen y Burgervan, a throng of cagouled Cardiffians weren't having their fun spoiled by a drop of rain, not when they'd ventured to the most northerly point in the known universe.

I was last at Llanidloes RFC to see Wales deservedly beaten by Georgia. Remember that? The smattering of unfortunates who had turned out were beyond even trying to be emotionally involved in what was unfolding on the screens. The game passed by in a subdued haze, like a funeral you've attended out of obligation.

Yesterday, the buzz was back. Boisterous youngsters, yet to be broken by years of disappointment, wore their expectations proudly. Sage old men narrowed their eyes and corrected the referee.

Warren Gatland's post-game remarks had none of the 'we've taken important learnings' complacency of the Pivac era. He was livid with Wales' capitulation in the final quarter and gave the impression that certain players would be hearing his condemnation in their nightmares for decades to come.

Obviously, we could and should have won. Cool your boots for a second, though, and consider that we apparently have two Welsh sides that are capable of winning at this level. If you'd have suggested that last year it would have elicited derision. It didn't matter how blind/thick/corrupt the referee was back then, we just weren't good enough. Now, when the friendless, whistle-happy bastard assumes we're idiotic enough to bring down a maul five metres from the England line, he's messing with the national zeitgeist.

You're going to watch the World Cup and you're going to allow yourself to imagine Wales winning it. You can tell yourself that you know better; you *do* know better. That eight-year-old inside though, is an insistent little thing. He's seen what Jac Morgan can do; he knows Liam Williams back in form, and he's ordered a jersey that fits.

A Cautionary Tale

23 July 2023

I didn't take a bus on Thursday for environmental reasons, nor because I thought it was likely to throw up a juicy metaphor for my column. Truthfully, I fancied a pint, so there is no need to thank me for my sacrifice. No, really, you're embarrassing me.

Get this, though. Trundling through the narrow road in Trehafod, we came to an unscheduled halt. The driver was leaning out of his window and trying to reason with the driver of a small car who was refusing to reverse a few yards to allow the bus through.

'I *can't* reverse, butt, I'm in a *bus*. I'm not allowed to if I wanted to!'

For 15 minutes the car driver refused to budge, inspiring amusement on the bus.

'It's fine, you carry on. Bomb-proof excuse for missing work this is.'

Eventually, with mouthed obscenities and unseemly hand gestures, he gave way and progress was restored.

On Friday morning the by-election results were in. It seemed a straightforward disaster for the Tories. The Lib Dems romped home in Somerton and Frome, while Labour unveiled its new Fisher-Price Keir as the victor in Selby and Ainsty. These results in reliably Tory seats confirm the fate awaiting Sunak & Co. at the General Election. 45 Conservative MPs are standing down before the election and they have an average age of 52, so the writing is on both sides of the wall, the windows, and carved into the front door with a Stanley knife.

Keir Sr, however, is not convinced. In Boris Johnson's former seat, Uxbridge and South Ruislip, the Tories hung on by 495 votes. That's a great result for Labour and shows that incumbent Tories need to fight every seat. By Friday morning, though, Starmer had concluded that Mayor Sadiq Khan should 'reflect' on his policy of expanding ULEZ charges to the outer London boroughs. This issue, it was confirmed by both Labour and Conservative canvassers, is what had stood in the way of a Labour victory. On Saturday morning he went further. At the National Policy Forum in Nottingham, he cited the failure to win Uxbridge as evidence that 'there is still a long way to go', concluding that, 'We are doing something very wrong if policies put forward by the Labour Party end up on each and every Tory leaflet. We've got to face up to that and learn the lessons.'

ULEZ is a major issue in Uxbridge because it's particular to that constituency. So, to extrapolate its effect on a General Election, particularly when you have conflicting polling *from the same night*, seems illogical. Starmer's discomfiture with Sadiq Khan's policy seems only to have arisen after the Uxbridge result and to have quickly gathered steam. ULEZ is a public health measure to address poor quality air. The policy was, in fact, mandated by the Conservative government as part of Transport for London's bail-out conditions during the pandemic.

In the black and white reductionism of the Culture War, however, it falls under 'green stuff' along with net zero and Just Stop Oil protestors. A recent Tory attack line has been to link Labour, and Starmer particularly, with these activists in the belief that their unpopularity with swing voters provides some leverage. It is perhaps perceived vulnerability to this line that guided Starmer's panicky response to results that seem to confirm Labour's trajectory towards government. Referencing Clause One of the party's constitution, he emphasised the primacy of winning power in his offer to the electorate. He signalled how far he's willing to go in order to achieve this by reflecting that, 'We've got to ask ourselves seriously – are our priorities the priorities of working people or are they just baggage that shows them we don't see the country through their eyes.'

Well, hold on, Sir Keir. Are we to equate the 'priorities of working people' with the views of less than 14,000 remaining Tory voters in a safe Tory constituency? I'm all for ambition but this is like Justin Bieber setting up shop at a Napalm Death convention and being horrified that his T-shirts don't sell out. These 14,000 voters have had Boris Johnson as their MP for the last eight years and yet still voted Tory. Personally, I wouldn't be looking to them for collective wisdom.

We are used to the Labour offer being progressively trimmed to suit the presumed values of middle England. Last week it was confirmed that the two-child cap on benefits would be retained, for instance. Caution is an understandable virtue in the wake of the governmental insanity we've endured for the last few years, but when it's translated to prevarication on environmental matters, it betrays a rootlessness which, over time, may come to haunt those who insist on it. Similarly, undermining the work of elected Labour politicians with devolved power risks alienating Labour support all over the UK.

The environment isn't available for compromise. It isn't the bond markets, or trade union leaders, or the EU Commission, it is a concrete reality with which we much reckon. Nearly every measure we have at our disposal is annoying and expensive for all of us. Recycling is annoying; airport surcharges are annoying; congestion charges are annoying; heat pumps will be extra annoying. Resultingly, many among us are happy to hear from politicians who make all of the above sound as if it is an optional luxury to appease fanatics.

A truly cautious response to the results on Thursday would have been to accept that an incoming Labour government is inevitable and begin to prepare the electorate for the principled decisions it will have to make. Chasing down every last Tory voter by evading reality is a short-sighted and reckless tactic that is storing up trouble for the future. Labour supporters pointed to the 893 Green votes that could have swung Uxbridge their way. They should reflect on how many potential Green voters had held their noses to vote Labour. Between metro mayors, the Senedd and the Scottish Parliament, there will be plenty of space for progressive opposition in the coming years, especially if the fundamental values upon which Labour politicians are elected to these seats of democracy is ignored by an Anglo-centric UK leadership.

We can sit in our 2007 Vauxhall Corsa shouting at the bus for as long as we like. The climate isn't reversing.

Camel-Haired Coutts

30 July 2023

Right, deep breath. Firstly, are you OK?[1] It's been an incredibly difficult time for all of us over the last couple of weeks. With the cost-of-living crisis, climate change turning southern Europe into an inferno, and the escalating threat of nuclear war over Ukraine, my plate was pretty full to start with. So, when news came through that NatWest Group had suggested downgrading Nigel Farage's Coutts account to the sort of high street arrangement you or I might use, I was knocked for six. A series of late-night conversations with my spiritual advisor saw me questioning my belief in a morally ordered universe. After all, how could a benign deity stand by while this simple son-of-a-stockbroker, who rose by dint of hard work to become a commodities trader, is laid low by the financial establishment?

The revolution will not spare you, Coutts! The people will not stand for their pint-swilling, fag-toting champion being treated as if he were us. He's not us; he's better than us but sometimes he pretends he is like us because he wants us to know he cares about us. That's the kind of man he is, you fiduciary bastards.

We thought you were the good guys, Coutts. We applauded your sensitivity in not making a scene when the Queen Mother accidentally bounced a £4 million cheque.

We know your game. Nigel warned us in 2019 that he'd be betrayed in his sermon at Trago Mills car park in Merthyr (£2.50 admission, bring your own chair). Little did he know that the

---

[1] This was Holly Willoughby's first line to *This Morning* viewers after Philip Schofield had run into trouble. Scripted empathy is my favourite kind.

knife between his shoulder blades would be wielded by His Majesty the King's personal bankers. Oh, perfidious Albion!

I can't keep this up.

Just as we've been granted an inevitably brief respite from having Boris Johnson's doings smeared in our faces over breakfast, back comes Farage to fill his narcissistic void. Those of you fastidious enough to avoid this nonsense should look away now, I salute you. For those who need a catch-up, Coutts closed the ranine populist's account and offered him a NatWest one. When questioned on it they said it was because he was skint, but it has emerged that it was because they thought he was too toxic to be associated with their brand.

Call me old-fashioned but I remember when it was less embarrassing to be broke than a pariah. For Farage, though, being a pariah is crucial to his business. If your schtick is to be a perpetually aggrieved avatar of discontent, then you need a supply of credible outrage to stay on the road. 'They' have done it to him yet again and they'll do it to you too, so vote for Nige. Or at least sign up for his investment scheme and become part of 'Britain's Great Wealth Revival'. After all, 'they' don't want you to be financially independent, that's why they're persecuting your pal Nige.

Who 'they' actually are never quite comes into focus. An unlikely and shifting coalition of Marxists, 'globalists', immigrants, climate scientists, bankers, and media organisations are ranged against the honest citizen, and the only way to salvation is through Nige. Just sign here and everything will be alright again.

Before LBC radio gave him the boot, I remember listening to one of his post-Brexit shows. Callers were discussing Theresa May's reluctance to force through a 'no deal' option and one rang up, seemingly frothing at the mouth, to warn that 'we' would settle it on the streets if she didn't acquiesce.

Farage's response was a masterpiece of nod-and-a-wink deniability.

'Ah, well we don't endorse direct action,' he cautioned. 'But it's interesting, isn't it? A lot of people are ringing up to say that. A lot of people.'

By such vagaries are insurrections launched, as Donald Trump demonstrated.

With an election looming, Farage will once again have the profile to address the terminally frustrated and whisper that their paranoid, fascist-adjacent notions are valid so the best way to advance them is by signing up to something that only costs a few quid.

Should malign hucksters be hung upside down from lamp posts in Trafalgar Square?

No, we don't endorse that.

But it's interesting, isn't it?

Where Angels Fear to Tread

13 August 2023

Came downstairs on Thursday morning to find the better angels of my nature halfway through a three-litre bottle of Electric White cider and making uncalled-for observations about Lorraine Kelly. Angrily. I turn off the telly.

'What do you think you are doing; how can I seek your moral affirmation after seeing you in this state? Do your trousers up.'

Lighting a Marlboro Red, an angel smiles and shakes his head.

'The game's up kiddo, there's no more we can do.' He looks around for seraphic solidarity and elicits a perfunctory rustle of wings from his brethren.

'I'm starting a podcast,' one chirps. 'An edgy take on the week's wrongdoing, co-presented with Moloch. We go hammer and tongs, but you could still imagine us having a pint together.'

'But, why?' I wail. 'Why would you leave me without guidance in this pitiless void?'

'They've started taking Lee Anderson seriously,' my former guardians chant in unison.

'God is dead, Lee has won.'

We've discussed Lee Anderson before, and people were quick to point out that people like him were best ignored. You'd think so, wouldn't you? Anderson's bigoted-uncle-at-Christmas schtick nauseates the vast majority of the electorate. It's aimed at a specific group of people: voters who, after everything we have gone through, are still open to the suggestion that another five years of Tory rule might be a good thing.

So, when he told the *Daily Express* this week that migrants should 'fuck off back to France' if they didn't fancy being housed on Legionnaire's-riddled barges, it sounded like another deliberate provocation from which the grown-ups at Number 10 could winkingly distance themselves.

'He might very well think that; we couldn't possibly comment.'

Except this time, they did comment. Confirming that Anderson's remark represented the government line, Justice Secretary Alex Chalk blanched only, he posed, at its 'salty language'.[1]

It is tempting to ascribe the shambles unfolding in UK politics to its ordered-from-Wish electoral system, or more widely to its so-good-we-don't-have-to-write-it-down Constitution. Because, if we're honest, we've never been that bothered about democracy around here, have we? Here we are, in 2023, allowing our affairs to be decided by the handful of bovine swing voters who are as easily biddable as your mom. Voting is not only optional and unworthy of a day off work, it's barely encouraged outside of competitive seats. Anybody participating in politics for reasons other than naked careerism is a 'crank', an 'extremist' and, eventually, an enemy of the people. Astride this constitutional Steely Dan perches the Monarchy, mocking our votes for their impotence: what the king giveth...

But no. The UK's democratic collapse is only its characteristically farcical version of an international crisis. In America, with its written Constitution, separation of powers, and

---

[1] This was genuinely shocking, I felt. The days when comically deranged extremists like Anderson can be safely dismissed are behind us. They are sent out to see what the electorate will tolerate and, frequently, the conclusion is 'anything'.

write-in ballots, the situation is worse still. If, as is likely, Joe Biden faces Donald Trump next November, the winner will send the loser to prison, probably for life. Political strategists on both sides will be playing a zero-sum game that offers no points for persuasion. There's nobody left to persuade. As MAGA hats chant and latte-sippers whine, the agency lies with people who can't be bothered. So, to overcome Biden's predicted lead, Trump needs to say things that will wake them up and propel them to the voting booth. Every day behind in the polls will be a day closer to incarceration, with the rhetoric ratcheted up accordingly.

So, let's hope he loses, eh? What's that, Flipper? He'll dispute the result from prison and his radicalised army of corndog-munching conspiracists will start a civil war?

Gosh, well perhaps on balance it might be best if Trump actually won. What did you say, Skippy? He'll rule like a king and jail his political opponents?

We're near the logical endpoint of a binary system that insults the plurality of its citizens by distorting their will to suit it. The only scenario beyond this is that losing candidates are executed.

We were, you will remember, taught that democracy was the source of Western supremacy in global affairs. Now, as China looks on with its planned economy and social credit system, it is collapsing beneath our feet.

The recently deceased Milan Kundera pondered how long it took for a tragic event to become a suitable topic for jokes.[2] The issue now is how long it takes the farcical to become tragic, and events suggest that interval is shortening.

It took a few years for Donald Trump to be taken seriously but his malign genius has filtered down to even the most hapless politicians the world over. *It doesn't matter what you say as long as enough people hear it.*

---

[2] Did you hear the one about the recently deceased Czech-French novelist?

241

Six months ago, Lee Anderson was a grotesque; figure of derision; a clown at the court. Now the court dances to his tune, and we know how that goes.

Barbenheimer

6 August 2023

Sensing that Mrs W was becoming jaded with my conversation about the 14 consecutive Beard Meats Food YouTube videos I'd watched, I thought I'd change things up a bit.

'Let's do Barbenheimer!' I suggest, artfully repositioning myself as a zeitgeist-surfing funster who knows how to enjoy himself.

'You'll have to wear pink.'

'Not a problem, can I borrow something?'

Nodding in disbelief, she leaves me to my eight-part documentary on Cuban cigars and puts in headphones to continue her Welsh lesson. She's so cute when she's learning things, yet also has the potential to ignite the atmosphere if underestimated.

Arriving at the Nantgarw Showcase, I join a long queue of cars.

'We'll be lucky to get a ticket,' I warn. 'It must be rammed.'

'You've joined the queue for the McDonalds drive-through,' my wife womansplains, visibly suppressing a smirk as I extricate us from Happy Meal purgatory.

I have issues with cinemas. Too many people, too loud, too emblematic of an exploitative consumer society that has numbed our collective capacity to experience art. Also, my first date was at Birmingham Odeon when I was 15. Suffice to say, I saw the end of *Big* with Tom Hanks, whilst my ra-ra-skirted companion supposedly visited the Ladies halfway through and never returned. I became a goth the next day.

So, my multiplex visits are few and far between. This is the first double-header I've seen since *Grease/Saturday Night Fever* in 1977, and my mum had to drag me off my spacehopper to go to that. I secure the tickets whilst Mrs W gets us both dustbin-sized containers of Diet Coke.

'Want some popcorn?' she enquires.

'It's not ketogenic,' I sniff.

The Showcase is advertising upcoming livestream concerts by André Rieu and Metallica. As every last morsel of human creativity is hoovered up by corporations and fed into their cultural meatgrinders, I confidently predict that we'll soon be able to see an AI-generated performance of Andreé Rieu *by* Metallica.

Alienation is a constituent part of the postmodern experience, I remind myself as we head into the virtually deserted auditorium for *Barbie.*

It's a properly weird film. Forget its title and look at the premise:

A movie made by a toy manufacturer about a still-popular plastic doll that posits it as a cause of society's decline but also its redeemer. Add in a modish meditation on gender and a side order of existentialism, then it's a wildly ambitious proposition.

Its willingness to 'fess up to Barbie's dubious role in gender relations can be explained in two ways, I reckon. Mattel, presumably, would say that this Maoist self-criticism evidences its alertness to the sophistication of 21st-Century customers. Your 2023 Barbie-owner is equipped with sufficient ironic layering to enjoy the product whilst remaining cognizant of its controversial past. She/he/they thrives in an ethically complex world and so does Barbie.

Alternatively, Mattel have assessed the nihilistic post-Trump landscape and concluded that they could have Barbie shoot a puppy on Fifth Avenue and their numbers would go up. *What* influential figures, be they presidents or dolls, do or say is less important than how many people pay attention. If someone can command an army of followers then that demonstrates the power of their will and, in an age of self-actuation, their virtue. Development of individual drive is, of course, Barbie's supposed example, so why shouldn't Mattel adapt it to the world as it is now? The casting of the stereotypically beautiful Margot Robbie is shrugged off by calling her 'stereotypical Barbie' and having narrator Helen Mirren chide the producers for doing it. Still, though, the plus-size, disabled, non-blonde Barbies are largely confined to group scenes and dance sequences. That's alright though, because Helen Mirren has lent her feminist credibility to a scripted acknowledgement of it.

The film is good fun as long as you don't think about it too much and, if you're voluntarily going to watch a two-hour advert for a doll, then being manipulated kinda comes as part of the deal.

Oppenheimer is up next, after a quick flat white in the cinema's onsite Costa. Kia-Ora is no longer a thing, apparently.

If *Barbie* is all about igniting the will, then *Oppenheimer* shows the pitfalls of projecting it too single-mindedly.

Because the horrifying climax of this story is known to the audience, director Christopher Nolan is freed from the need to build tension. The plotting is tortuously complex, with timelines overlapping so frequently that it's an effort to piece together what is happening when. Startling visuals and superb performances from Cillian Murphy and Emily Blunt distract from a substantive deficit at the film's heart.

We get Tom Conti as Einstein but very little actual physics. There's stuff scribbled on blackboards and cameos for Heisenberg and Nils Bohr, but no sense of the grandeur of their thinking.

We see the damage that politics does to Oppenheimer, but no space is afforded to a Japanese perspective.

Back home, Mrs W has to suffer the verbal consequences of

245

my brain being exposed to too many narratives. It finally short circuits in exhaustion and peace is restored.

Watching Beard Meats Food again after she's gone to bed, I reflect that all this stuff, whether it's building a world-dominating toy brand, or developing science to interrogate the universe is, ultimately, 'ways of slowly dying' as Larkin put it.[1]

We have some years on a planet and however loudly or impressively we fill them, the denouement is the same. *Barbie* might conceivably inspire a youngster to excel at physics. That might, in isolation, turn out not to be for the greater good.

In the grand scheme of things, it's better to direct your will towards eating a 100oz steak within a 45-minute time window. If you fail to appreciate the consequences, it isn't the end of the world.

---

[1] Work that GCSE, Ben!

How to Watch Wales Lose

29 August 2023

Work, work, work, work, work, SATURDAY, something involving relatives or garden centres. That's the rhythm of it and we have a right to expect some relief on the one day we get. Joy, though, is something different, and it doesn't care what the scoreboard says.

Think back on the games you've watched and remember the shapes of those days. Anyone who hasn't used a Welsh loss as justification for reckless abandon afterwards has missed the point. When the game starts, it's daylight and you might have a spring in your step. I didn't have much of one in mine slogging up the hill to Penrhys from Tylorstown. The only rational reason for climbing this hill is to get buried, so crack on.

Two drinks in, I'm making the case that Tylorstown RFC should govern the valley. Nothing works up here, not unless people go out of their way, and the rugby club goes further than anything else. It radiates warmth past the cemetery and down into the larger, uglier valley where my pal Phil caught his bus.

'Alright, Phil?'

How does the independence movement make an accommodation with deeply held socialist convictions? We may never know, because soon enough the game is under way, so shush, Ben.

I don't know what we expect, really. Three months ago, rugby in Wales was dead, wasn't it? All dreams were cancelled, and we were to accept that our collective fecklessness had been our undoing. There was a terrible reckoning to come, and all future Saturdays would be coloured by shame. Nye Bevan had

247

signed to run a Division Three health service in Japan.

I'm alone in predicting a Welsh win, as I often am. The spectrum of opinion at our table reaches indigo with Phil's vote for a 15-point loss, which I dismiss as clinical avoidance. Evidently, he's inoculating himself against disappointment by assuming the pain in advance. Then again, how often at 50, do you get to be kid in the room, bouncing around with absurd dreams? I'll take that as a win.

It's in the dark, after the game, when you see what you're all about. When the singers are hauling PA systems into rugby clubs, and bouncers are cracking their knuckles on St Mary's Street, more nervous than they dare admit, that's when the decision is made. We've lost, so what are we going to make of the evening?

There was nothing to risk a night in the cells about this afternoon. South Africa are way better than England, but they had to work to prove it. Those 15 Welsh players will never play together again because that wasn't the point of the game. It's all good, Taulupe is on the mend. We haven't peaked too early, or something.

One of the innumerable pleasures of life in Rhondda Fach is how dark it gets at night. When you're walking down it you can appreciate your solitude in the dim glow of council negligence. With Trebanog glittering above you and Tylorstown tip menacing to your left, Ponty might as well be Monte Carlo. It's the perfect setting for reflection, a privilege really.

So, when I reach home, I'm bursting to tell my wife how great the club was, why it's what life's all about. She's smiling at me indulgently, I don't drink often nowadays. A smile can really hit you, can't it?

'You know I love you, right?'

'You've transferred your allegiance, have you?'

'What do you mean?'

248

'From Wales to me.'

'Sort of. Mean it though.'

'Go to bed.'

The Age of Anxiety

21 May 2023

At the end of a large dinner, it seemed like a good idea to hop on the short boat ride from Lipsi to Patmos the next day. We'd fallen into an easy familiarity with the smaller island, the paths to its pretty coves, the restaurants with their attentive cats, and the bakery that was open all night and sold fags. It's not enough to be happy somewhere, though, is it? Not when you've paid for it and time is short. You must *make the most of things* and wring all the juice from your precious time away from work.

Just over there, in Patmos, John the Theologian wrote the Book of Revelation in a cave that you can visit and have a look round. Now, I'm not a religious person, but I went to a Christian school, so read the whole Bible before I was 10, and that particular bit does pack a punch. For sure, Bill Hicks would have gone if he was this close. I mean, the Book of Revelation is trippier than listening to Syd Barrett's solo output after five dried grams of Powys's finest at dawn on Midsummer's Day. *The actual cave*, where the Dude of the New Testament saw the Four Horsemen of the Apocalypse! C'mon Mrs W, we've got to catch that boat....

Plans hatched after retsina and tsipouro on the islands tend to take on a tarnished aspect the next morning. Awakening to lapping waves and a blinding headache, I reach for Mrs W to find her stoically packing her tote bag for the trip I'd evangelised for so effectively the night before. Not for the first time, I've snookered myself here: I'm pretty sure she doesn't want to go, and I don't now, but I've made such an erudite case for it, quoting scripture and everything, that I'd look like a nob if I roll over and go back to sleep.

On the boat over it's okay, I suppose. The swell, wind, and endless outlines of mythical-looking islands can get a bit too much though. There's only so many times you can imagine the approach of a trireme before you revert to your phone. I catch up on the news. Well marvellous, the seemingly self-replicating army of dicksplash self-publicists who, unbidden, infect my Twitter feed with their infantile, Fascist-adjacent drivel are holding a conference under the banner of 'National Conservatism'. Barely holding on to a hastily devoured *spanokopita*, I disembark on Patmos wondering how the hell the UK could have got here so fast and without anybody setting themselves on fire in outrage.

We amble over to a café to acclimatise. Mrs W is understandably confused that I don't seem to be enjoying my big day out quite as much as might be expected, but in that moment, over a Freddo Cappuccino with the sun slanting in across the harbour, I'm coping.

So, we head off up the hill to what the Greeks call the Cave of the Apocalypse. You'd probably skip up here but I'm a heavy, leaden shambles nowadays, whose elasticity is confined to sentence structure, so you'll have to imagine my lumbering progress towards the spot where humanity was first imagined to be a self-propelling agent of its own destruction.

It hasn't been particularly hot, but in Greece, as in Wales, the weather is changeable and heading up the hill, away from the cool looking bay, the sun begins to thrum a little. The traffic system on the way to Bristol airport is really confusing when you're driving in the dark. I hope that I didn't trip any speed cameras because if I get any more points that might affect work and people don't want to hire you when you're gone 50, plus what would I do? When I get home there could be five tickets waiting for me on the mat, sent out automatically by machines. The lactic acid is building in my legs but that's good because you're building muscle strength, aren't you? Why on earth do they keep banging on about Philip Schofield and Meghan Markle when people are starving? It

251

makes no sense. My ears are whistling, is that what you get when you are having a stroke? I read that somewhere. Keep walking, faster, faster, faster....

About 50 yards shy of the cave I'm overwhelmed, clawing at my stomach as it fills up with cortisol and frantically pressing my fingers into my neck to check my pulse. Sinking.

Opposite me, high up on this mountain ridge, is the driveway entrance to the Patmos hospital. It should be a comfort, really, if, this time I am actually having a heart attack, instead of another stupid, pitiful anxiety episode, then some Greek doctor in there will obey Hippocrates over Brexit and set me right. But the anxious mind doesn't work like that. The hospital is there because those are the places people die in and they are going to cart me in there from this pine-scented, silent paradise and my heart will bleed out leaving my son under-parented, my book unfinished and that will be it.

Mrs W catches up with me and instructs me to sit carefully on a rock.

'Tell me five things you can see.'

'The sea, some pine trees, stones, my hands, your face.'

She hands me a water bottle, massages my shoulders, and repeats the exercise through my remaining four senses until I stabilise.

Eventually, I'm steady enough to resume our original plan and we jitter down to Happy John's cave. Past the gift shop entrance, where the bored custodian glances up from his phone to take our six Euros, we press on to the site itself. An elderly, bearded priest, perhaps the unhappiest man I've ever seen, leaps up as I enter and looks accusatorily at the phone in in my hand. He bars my progress with his robed leg until I put it into my pocket before sitting back down and performatively poring over his large, leatherbound book.

A devout woman cries and touches the walls.

I suppose we are all having some kind of day.

Acknowledgements

I've floated on an ocean of goodwill as I've been writing these pieces. The supportive atmosphere for writers here in Wales is uniquely generous and has lent me the confidence to take risks I wouldn't have dared to imagine when I started.

Nation.Cymru is the best outlet in Wales. I'm indebted to Jon Gower for taking a chance on me in the first place and encouraging belief; to Mark Mansfield for wise guidance and establishing such a vibrant environment, and to Sarah Morgan Jones for dealing with my anxieties as the columns were put together. If you enjoy them, I urge you to seek out the online versions where you can find Sarah's photo choices and progressively spicier subheadings.

I didn't write these pieces believing that they'd have any extended life, and their appearance here is thanks to the kind initiative of Chris Jones at Cambria Books.

I should take a moment to genuflect before Andrew 'Real Ting' Davies: the patron saint of Welsh satirists.

Finally, I must gather all the admiration I have for my brilliant wife, Susie. Her contributions include, but are far from limited to: proofreading the writing and kindly conveying where I've ceased to make a lick of sense; enduring hours of political 'conversation' that is, in reality, me rehearsing a column; cheerfully allowing me to steal things she has said; tolerating my presenting her as a fictional character for general amusement; feeding me; gently alerting me that I have my T-shirt on inside out, and making life worth living.

Milton Keynes UK
Ingram Content Group UK Ltd.
UKHW041914211123
433012UK00004B/48